The Harley Chronicles

Everything I Learned about My Marriage on the Back of a Harley

Pirri,

Hang on for the Ride!

It's worth the Trip.

Sarah Huxford

Sarah Huxford

WESTBOW
P R E S S®
A DIVISION OF THOMAS NELSON
& ZONDERVAN

Scripture taken from the Holy Bible, NEW INTERNATIONAL VERSION®. Copyright © 1973, 1978, 1984, 2011 by Biblica, Inc. All rights reserved worldwide. Used by permission. NEW INTERNATIONAL VERSION® and NIV® are registered trademarks of Biblica, Inc. Use of either trademark for the offering of goods or services requires the prior written consent of Biblica US, Inc.

Scripture quotations are from The Holy Bible, English Standard Version® (ESV®), copyright © 2001 by Crossway, a publishing ministry of Good News Publishers. Used by permission. All rights reserved.

WestBow Press books may be ordered through booksellers or by contacting:

WestBow Press
A Division of Thomas Nelson & Zondervan
1663 Liberty Drive
Bloomington, IN 47403
www.westbowpress.com
1 (866) 928-1240

ISBN: 978-1-5127-2324-3 (sc)
ISBN: 978-1-5127-2326-7 (hc)
ISBN: 978-1-5127-2325-0 (e)

Library of Congress Control Number: 2015920511

Print information available on the last page.

WestBow Press rev. date: 01/04/2016

Acknowledgments

I would like to thank my husband for encouraging me the whole ride and allowing me to tell our story in this crazy way. To you, I say, "Honey, I'd do it all over again. Every mile with you is worth the trip!"

A special thank you must go out to my three sons and their wives, my three daughters, for not letting me quit on this book project. To you, I say, "I am inspired by your marriages. I love how you love giving!"

I would never have made it without Lindsay Huxford and her formatting skills, Laura Driver and her brilliant editing, *or* my two sweet sisters: Kathy Brownell, with her scriptural wisdom, and Becky Jackson, with her masterful study questions. To you, I say, "Thanks for walking this road with me. Your contributions turned this book into something I like."

To my friend Renee Ryan, I say, "Thank you for being the first person to call me a writer. Your encouragement won't be forgotten."

To my other two siblings, Bill and Mary, who never found anything wrong with the book in the first place, I say, "I like your kind of critique."

Dedication

This book is dedicated to the women of all ages at Compassion Christian Church. Their questions were my inspiration. When my sweet sisters in the Lord saw me appear in black leather, or heard (usually from the pulpit) that I had been riding on a Harley, I was asked many times, "Who are you and what have you done with our preacher's wife?"

Contents

CHAPTER ONE

Harley and Me

"Jump on! Let's go for a ride."

—Him

We had hit a new stage in our marriage that friends told us would be wonderful. It was the stage where the kids were all gone and the dog had died. Supposedly, a whole new freedom would be ours. The only problem was that having our kids gone was the worst thing I had ever faced, and our dog Bucky still lived on in all of our hearts. Bucky was our special golden retriever who had traveled with us the whole trip, every trip, from the time my youngest was in preschool. The first day he met his boys, Bucky chased everything they could throw as well as the red shoelaces attached to our youngest son's feet. He followed their every step until the time came when his only job was to sit in the driveway and watch them each leave for college. As you might expect, the dog was not replaceable.

We received extensive advice on how to enjoy this new phase of life and how to make the most of our new freedom. The dominant theme centered on leveraging this opportunity for renewing our closeness, fellowship, and relationship. With the boys gone and a new dog out of the question, I assumed that the "relationship renewing" was going to be with my husband. I threw myself into this opportunity with all of my usual preconceived ideas. I knew exactly how it was going to be with just the two of us. I could almost hear the song playing in the air as I planned. My husband lovingly tells me that I am a woman with a script in my brain, and he will attest to the fact that life is much happier for me when everyone is *on script*. He once suggested I just give him his lines early enough so he could get them right. I, of course, got my feelings hurt. I hadn't a clue what he was talking about.

Enter Harley. What or who was this new intruder into the "just the two of us" time? In all honesty, I was not very excited to see this new direction my husband's affection was taking. I heard about Harley way before I saw him, and I wasn't impressed. I definitely didn't like the look he put in my husband's eye. So, me being me, a woman who lives with a script, I had a bad attitude the first day Harley roared into our lives. He entered with a half a dozen of my husband's smiling friends. The whole motley crew looked

2

at me as if I should have realized this was one of the *best days* … in the history of days … *ever*. My heart instantly turned against our new friend Harley.

I might have felt bad about my attitude if he had been a horse, but he was a machine. A shiny, candy-apple red Harley motorcycle. The term *iron horse* was thrown around with the same sense of rugged individualism as *modern-day cowboy*. I think I was supposed to get misty eyed as I pictured Harley and my husband venturing across the great American West, much as our forefathers had, to see this great land of ours. Sounded noble, I guess. But I still wasn't getting it. When the excitement died down and all of the friends were gone, I was not at all happy to hear those inevitable words: "Jump on! Let's go for a ride."

This may sound too dramatic, but I need to point out that those words changed my life. I didn't realize it at the time. My initial response, again with an attitude, was something subtle, like, "I'm not getting on that thing! Are you crazy?" However, as usual whenever my husband has that look in his eye, I gave in. No point in arguing with the charming look. It gets me every time. With fear and trembling, I faced my first ride.

After that one ride, I knew Harley was going to be an established part of this new phase of our marriage. He had not only found a place in my husband's heart; he had captured mine as well. This didn't change the fact that I had to get a few things straight before Harley and I could coexist compatibly. I went to the garage that night, and we had a little talk. "You can't have him all to yourself, you know." On this point I would not relent. "I get to be a part of some of your time together. So you better take good care of me."

Our first official trip was to beautiful Sea Island, Georgia. On that initial voyage, I found I was well cared for, both by my husband and by Harley. From my secure spot on the back of this motorcycle (a spot we now just call *the throne*), I discovered the joy of riding! I was overwhelmed with the unexpected exuberance that thrilled beneath my skin as the combination of wind and speed swept away the stress of the day. The simplicity of sitting there, not saying a word, but still very much "just the two of us" watching the beauty rush by was my undoing. I said something to my husband that day that I have said on every Harley ride since … and with the same bad grammar: "Thanks for bringing me!"

And he always replies, "Thanks for coming."

We started our friendship that day, Harley and I.

From that point on, I started making a spot for Harley in our lives and our home. I personally made his part of the garage welcoming, complete with black-and-white tiles and a sign that reads "Harley Parking *Only*—All Others Will Be *Crushed*." We named him Big Red, and that seemed to seal the deal. He was now officially a member of the family.

Lessons Learned from the Back of a Harley

The first lesson from our early Harley days was that *I need to do my part*. This lesson will always stay with me for one simple reason: it shocked me. After all, I thought I always did my part. When I thought about my marriage for the last few decades, I never thought, *Sarah, I wish you would do your part*. Now, admittedly, there was another name that I whispered quietly in prayer, asking God to tell "him" to do his part, but I never I mentioned my own name.

My husband's name is Cam, short for Campbell. As you read about him in the *Harley Chronicles*, he will only be called *husband* or *him*. However, as we enter these lesson sections together, I want you to get to know us both. We wholeheartedly believe God intends our marriage to last a lifetime. Because of that belief, we take the job of strengthening our marriage seriously. That includes evaluating how our marriage is doing on a regular basis. When it came to the evaluation process, I couldn't see anything I needed to do. But I could always make a list of some things Cam could work on.

Those of you who are more insightful than I am can already see the problem. Yes, I was living in denial, but I blame our culture, really. Oh no, now I'm playing the blame game. I do think, however, that it has become very trendy to fix our husbands. We proceed with our lists and set of goals for "all that he could be" if he really put his mind to it. We then sit and talk for hours with our friends about how he is not quite living up to his potential.

I think now is a good time to remind ourselves of the number one truth about marriage. *Marriage is a primary human relationship.* It was planned by God from the very beginning. It was introduced into man's experience as the first form of human companionship. They had a relationship with God first, then as husband and wife. All other human relationships were experienced as secondary to the first two. God illustrated His plan by introducing this relationship early on in Adam and Eve's existence. *Relationship,* by its very definition, is a two-way street. There must be two participating parties. As soon as God had two people, He started building relationships.

We know marriage is God's plan, and it is good. However, on the very human side of this experience, two people connecting for a lifetime of companionship is challenging. Now would be a good time to remind ourselves of another truth concerning the marriage relationship: you can only fix yourself. I think this is possibly the number two truth to embrace when walking daily in a marriage. First, God planned this; and second, *you can only be responsible for changing you.*

It was a good day when I realized that if I really wanted a relationship that was growing closer and deeper, I needed to do my part. I have asked Cam to understand my world many times over the years, and he has tried (with great effort) to do this—and still does. Let's talk a little more truth here, girls. To put it nicely, we women are ever-changing organisms, and it's not that easy to figure out where we are emotionally at any given moment. In all honesty, by the time our men figure us out, we may have changed. We can change seasonally, monthly, or by the decade. In fact, I might have to ask the Lord about this last change when I get to heaven. *Who* ever thought menopause was a good idea? Was this really the way it was supposed to work? Cam helped me with a man's analogy. He said I was an ever-moving target that, although it was difficult to hit, was worth the effort. I, on the other hand, thought I had *him* figured out and didn't need to work at it. What a sad contrast between our responses. I had taken his stable nature for granted. I had some work to do. How long had it been since I entered his world?

It may take a little effort to understand our husbands' world, but it will be worth it. The alternative is very scary to me: living side by side physically, yet still very separate emotionally. We had seen too many marriages that had settled for this option. I didn't want ours to be one of them. I had to answer some important questions: Do I really know the dreams my husband has and the desires of his heart? Do I still care?

What do you need to make friends with in your husband's life? I pray that it's not as big and scary as a Harley, but it may be something equally daunting. Is there a part of his world where he invited you to come along for the trip but you just wouldn't go there? It may be a fishing pole or a golf club, but if we women make it the enemy, it will be our loss. You may be closing the door to something very special. Leave it open, and it could allow you to know something beautifully new about your husband, yourself, and your marriage.

Bible Backup:

The Bible gives quite a bit of insight into the marriage relationship. As Christians, we are not left in the dark to wander around, hoping we will bump into the right answers for our marriage. In this day and time, you can find a myriad of sources, from books to DVD studies, that will give good information on marriage. You will find sources listed at the end of each chapter. This book is not trying to be another in a long line of good advice … but to be a reminder that God can speak to us in unusual ways. My prayer for you as you process this book is that you will experience it in one of three ways. The first way is to read the book just for you; if God speaks to you, write it down and answer the questions that are presented. This is an ideal way to remember the things He shows you about yourself. The second possibility is that you will read some of this book as a couple. Cam and I have found that sometimes all we need is a common language to talk about the issues in our marriage. Reading the same book often gives us that tool. The third opportunity will be for you to gather a group of women together for the next eight weeks and talk about what it looks like to do your part in your marriages. As you process the topics that come up each week and spend time unpacking the Scripture in this section, God will remind you that He did not leave you without help—or hope.

So let's dig in ...

Design: Read Genesis 2:20–25

The first Scripture passage that talks about marriage is in the very first book of the Bible. As you spend some time reading and unpacking this Scripture, see if you can put into your own words what God's intention was for man and woman. The word *design* sums up this passage for me. Marriage was God's design. He had a plan for man and woman that He knew would work. He let Adam wander around alone for a while so he would know that God's design was perfect.

Biblical Fact Check

Read the following passage. Genesis 2:7, 8, and 18–25

7 Then the Lord God formed a man from the dust of the ground and breathed into his nostrils the breath of life, and the man became a living being. 8 Now the

Lord God had planted a garden in the east, in Eden; and there he put the man he had formed.

18 The Lord God said, "It is not good for the man to be alone. I will make a helper suitable for him."19 Now the Lord God had formed out of the ground all the wild animals and all the birds in the sky. He brought them to the man to see what he would name them; and whatever the man called each living creature, that was its name. 20 So the man gave names to all the livestock, the birds in the sky and all the wild animals. But for Adam no suitable helper was found. 21 So the Lord God caused the man to fall into a deep sleep; and while he was sleeping, he took one of the man's ribs and then closed up the place with flesh. 22 Then the Lord God made a woman from the rib he had taken out of the man, and he brought her to the man.

23 The man said,"This is now bone of my bones and flesh of my flesh; she shall be called 'woman,' for she was taken out of man." 24 That is why a man leaves his father and mother and is united to his wife, and they become one flesh.

25 Adam and his wife were both naked, and they felt no shame.

1. What word does God use to describe the kind of *being* He created when He created Adam?_____ Does He call any of his other creatures *living* beings? Why does he make this distinction?_____

_____

2. What is it that God says is *not good* about the situation of the man whom He has made?_____

_____

3. How does the man come to realize that there is something missing in his life?_____

_____

4. Marriage is a *relationship*. List God's specific actions during the creation of the woman that illustrate this truth._____

_____

If God's design was perfect, why is there not a world full of perfect marriages?

Cam had a GPS that worked really well. He loved the way it was designed, and he found that he didn't like to venture too far from home without it. In his usual brilliance, my husband figured out a way to attach the device to Big Red. Everything was great! One day, however, while traveling sixty-five miles an hour down the highway, the GPS flew off and shattered into pieces. Cam picked up all of the pieces he could find and brought it home. I said maybe it wasn't designed to ride on a motorcycle. I'm not sure he appreciated that observation because he had a plan. He was going to send it back to the company for a new one. Now when I say my husband is good with words, that's an understatement. By the time he finished talking to the customer service representative about how they were his favorite company in the world and they made the best product on the market and he was shocked that their unit malfunctioned, fell off, and broke, their answer was, "Our product is not designed to ride on a Harley, but send it back. We'd love to give you a new one, Mr. Huxford. You're such a great customer." That's called grace.

It's wise to remember that when we don't have any regard for the manufacturer's instructions, life is dangerous. There is a whole world full of marriages racing down the highway, not following the plans of the Designer. Some of you may already have found yourselves in marriages that are broken to pieces. I love Cam's GPS story. Even though my husband didn't deserve it, his story had a happy ending.

Do you realize you have a Master Designer who knows exactly how you are created and what is best for you? He is waiting for you to pick up the pieces of your marriage and hand them back to Him. He's the only one who can put them back together the right way. You have a chance to follow the manual this time.

Is you GPS broken?

Do you want to fix it?

- *Step one is desiring a closeness with your husband.*

- *Step two is figuring out who he really is, what makes him tick, and honoring that.*

- *Step three is choosing to do your part every day, doing the work necessary for this relationship.*

Desire: Read Genesis 3:16–20

What do you think it means when the verse says about Eve, "Your desire will be for your husband?"

The words *design* and *desire* are the two words God used to get through to me in my marriage. The first speaks to the hope God intended for us in the perfect world He created for us. The second word reminds us that in the fallen world after sin entered, life is going to take some work. I'm not crazy about this. My marriage, however, is worth the effort. I have the privilege of waking up every morning and choosing to do my part.

Marriage is still God's perfect plan, and His design is flawless. I am flawed, and I need the hand of the Creator in my marriage. I think He told me to spend some more time on that Big Red Harley when my husband invites me along. To be really truthful, I'm always surprised that my husband still wants me to come along. After all, I'm a lot more trouble for him than I'm worth. It would be much easier to ride alone … but that's another story for another chapter.

Personal Fact Check

- *Marriage Truth #1: Marriage is a primary human relationship. What does this mean?*

- *Marriage Truth #2: You can only* fix *yourself. You can only be* responsible *for* changing *you. Why is this a struggle in marriage?*

- *The first lesson Harley taught me was, "I have to do my part."*

Journal for a moment about what doing "my part" might mean for you in your marriage specifically.

_____

_____

_____

Group Discussion Questions:

1. Can you remember a time when your ideas of "relationship building," "renewed fellowship," and "just the two of us" were obviously not in sync with your husband's? Was there a time when you realized you weren't even in the same hemisphere?

Remember a conversation that revealed this great chasm between two great minds.

2. What intruder threatens your vision of "just the two of us" in your life? Describe him/her/it. How does it make you feel? Why do you see it as a threat?

3. Was there a point in time when your husband asked you to be a part of his hobby, interest, passion, vision, or dream? How did you respond? Do you wish you had responded differently? Explain.

4. Do you view your mate as simple or complex? Explain why. Be honest. What if you are wrong?

5. Do you know what your husband's dreams are? What makes him tick? How does his brain work and how does he process things? What makes him feel valued and important?

6. Have you experienced an emotional drift in your marriage? Think back. Where do you think this started?

7. What contemporary cultural ideas are at odds with God's design for marriage?

8. What do we as women do to sabotage this design? What if you *really* gave up trying to be in control?

9. Think about the intruder in your marriage. Describe the difference between tolerating it and embracing it.

10. How would this manifest itself in your life? Make a list of words under each choice that shows your possible actions, attitudes, and outcomes.

Recommended Reading: *The Meaning of Marriage* by Tim Keller

Biker's Trip Stats
&
Passenger's Log

*Starting/Ending Destination: Savannah, GA to Sea Island, GA (89.7 miles)

*Best Highways to Ride: GA 25/US 17S

Savannah, GA

*Don't Miss This:

Savannah, GA ... home of the Savannah Jazz Festival!

Historic Savannah Trolley Tour

Forsyth Park

City Market (shopping and restaurants)

River Street

Lucas Theater

Savannah Theater

First Saturdays on the River

*Great Places to Eat:

The Shell House

Vinnie Van Go Go's Pizza

Lady and Son's

The Pink House

Sapphire Grill

We'll Be Back!

Mrs. Wilkes's Boarding House Restaurant: This place is a true Southern experience! You will arrive to find the lunch line out the door and around the block. When you get to go inside, the magic begins. It's like stepping back in time. You are seated at a big boarding-house table sized to fit a crowd. Your party is seated together with several other groups all around the same table. If you are in the first seating of the day, someone will pray and bless the food, and you're off. Bowls full of vegetables and side dishes start arriving to be passed around family style. Platters of meats and baskets of warm bread keep coming, accompanied by, of course, lots of sweet tea.

When you're finished, don't forget to take your plate to the kitchen and thank the cook. It's a delightful experience. We've been several times ... and we'll be back.

Richmond Hill, GA

*Don't Miss This:

Fort Mcallister State Park

> Richmond Hill ... home of
> the Seafood Festival

St. Simons Island, GA

*Don't Miss This:

> St. Simons Island, GA ... home of the
> Sunshine Festival Arts & Crafts Show

St. Simons Lighthouse

Fort Frederica National Monument

*Great Places to Eat:

Barbara Jeans (famous for Crab Cakes)

Blackwater Grill (featured on Food

Network's *Diners, Drive-ins & Dives*)

Fourth of May Café (great breakfast)

So We Hear ... If you are looking for barbecue done the "old school" way, visit **Southern Soul Barbeque** in St. Simons Island. They were featured on Food Network's *Diners, Drive-ins & Dives!*

Delightful Detours:
Brunswick, GA–Sidney Lanier
Bridge (Great View)

Worth The Trip: Barbara Jean is famous for miles around for her crab cakes. But my husband says the restaurant's best-kept secret is the shrimp and grits. Cam Quote: "It's the ugliest food you can't wait to eat again. We'll be back!"

CHAPTER TWO

The Harley Swagger

"Look at me! I'm on the back of a Harley."

—Me

Not only had Big Red become a part of our family, but he was bringing us into his family as well. The Harley family tree has many branches ... with some more colorful than others. Of course, being a newcomer, I'll be the first to admit that I didn't know much about the family traditions. That first week, I was given a helpful initiation into some Harley-approved actions that proved to be very important.

Riding proudly past my friend down the street, I couldn't help but give her a wave that said, "Look at me! I'm on the back of a Harley! Can you believe that?" If you want to picture this wave, you can imagine my right hand up close to my right ear, waving back and forth madly. I felt it necessary to draw attention to my face as she might not know it was me, what with the helmet and all. It might have been hard to recognize me, and I didn't want her to miss it. There were also occasions when passing someone

I might know that I even added the little pointing gesture for emphasis that said, "Look! It's really me!" My husband found this breach of motorcycle etiquette serious enough to give me *The Talk* about the proper Harley wave. If you are like me and are unaware of what this looks like, I will explain. Now picture the left hand loosely draped over the left knee and two fingers moving in a hardly perceptible relaxed wave.

Down low. Got it!

But what about the poor neighbors on the other side of the street? What were they going to think? The only options are that: 1) I can't see them (maybe they'll understand it's the helmet); or 2) I'm now stuck up. Just when I was thinking that the only option was to try to get them on the way back … problem solved! I learned the nod. To the right side of the street, you give the chin lift. Again, don't try this with too much enthusiasm. After I learned these two things, I couldn't help but feel a little more a part of the family.

In an attempt to help acclimate me to life on the road, Cam and Big Red made sure our trips those first weeks were not too far from home. One such memorable trip, referred to now as the *bridge run,* was our first big adventure. To this day, if my husband disappears without telling me after a taxing day of meetings, I know he and Big Red have taken off on the *bridge run*. The first bridge was the Herman Talmadge Bridge over the Savannah River. The view was wonderful, and the wind at the top took me on a ride that definitely got my blood pumping. We arrived in South Carolina, but then the following series of bridges circled us back home to Georgia.

The other bridges were not as spectacular as the Talmadge Bridge. Some were low and almost at water level, but the views from the back of Big Red were unbelievable. The grassy marshes interrupted only by shiny ribbons of water went on for miles. The sun was setting, and we saw the color of the water change from golden yellow to a rosy peach before our eyes. My husband pointed out sights he didn't want me to miss and shared a beauty with me that I didn't even know existed within ten miles of our house. I was hit with an unexpected awe and wonder that will stay with me a lifetime.

As we stopped to check something on the bike, I found myself looking at my husband in a new way. I was overwhelmed with all he had taken time to share with me about the land and the wildlife we had passed. This is the same land we had lived in and driven by for twenty-five years, and yet it was the first time I had witnessed those haunting scenes. I tried to mention a few thoughts that I could put into words … something about the *new* beauty I had experienced that day in our *old* home … but when my words wouldn't suffice, I just said, "Thanks for bringing me."

It was at this stop that I saw *it* reappear. *The swagger* was back (maybe it was the boots). Now, my husband had a walk when I met him that could only be described as a swagger. I know this because I sat in groups of girls that discussed this openly and tried to find another name for it. Each adjective offered up was followed by, "No that's not it. It's a swagger. No other word for it—a swagger." This walk found its source in the attitude he had about life. To say the least, this swagger changed my life. Well, let's just say it was one of hundreds of things that let me know who he was and made me sure that I wanted to know this man for a lifetime.

If being on a Harley gave him back his swagger, I was all for it. Many people have asked me what could possibly be the appeal of riding on Big Red. When trying to put it into words, I just say it's the kind of fun that makes you feel like a college kid again. I hope it makes my husband feel like he did when he met me. I know it has allowed me to remember the man I first loved. He's probably kept the swagger all along … I just forgot to watch for it.

I love the lessons I'm learning from the back of a Harley. Here's the most important one. When it comes to renewing a relationship, whether with your husband or the Lord Jesus, the Bible tells us to return to our first love and do the things that we did in the beginning. How long had it been since I really looked at my husband and saw the man I married?

I've seen the swagger come back at different times in our marriage, and sometimes I have seen it reappear in the little boys who share his genetics. I could look across two soccer fields and see a miniature body walking my way, face not yet distinguishable, and my friend would say, "That's a Huxford there. I may not know which one, but I know it's a Huxford." I would just smile and agree. Through the years, we have changed the name of that endearing walk to the *Huxford Shuffle,* but I know (and my sons' wives know) that it's really a swagger.

Lessons Learned from the Back of a Harley

From the Old Testament, when God called Himself husband, to the New Testament Gospels, when Jesus tried to tell the disciples that the bridegroom was with them, until the final pages of the Book of Revelation, the theme is clear. Marriage, the most intimate of human relationships, is the picture God uses to teach us about His love. Jesus, the master teacher, always painted unforgettable pictures with His words and stories. Marriage is one of those pictures. I want a clear picture in my heart and head that isn't blurred by my own selfishness. There is too much riding on this thing called marriage to just do it my way. So I have been spending a good bit of time lately asking God how to do it His way.

We will make several stops as we go through God's Word on the topic of marriage. In the lesson for this week, our stop may surprise you. God is often put in a harsh light, depicted as demanding and controlling. However, in this Scripture, we see His heart of love. The character giving us the clearest *picture* of God is the bridegroom in Song of Solomon. We will see that the loving heart of the bridegroom longs to be chosen. He will never force his love

27

on his bride. If there is a husband in your life, he wears that role because you chose him to be your bridegroom at some point. When the Bible calls us to honor that role, just remember, you *chose* him. Yes, I'm going to repeat it ... he was a *choice*. Your *choice*. I know you may get tired of this word before it's all over.

We *practice* making this choice for years before we ever actually make the final monumental decision. Let me illustrate. I was fifteen when I was sure I'd seen the man for me. He rode up on his horse, and his blue eyes looked out from under his cowboy hat, and I was hooked. He lived close to me and said he was just riding around. Then he said, "I'll be back," and I said "I'll be here." It was a long and meaningful conversation and spurred many hours of thought racing through my head.

Then there was the boy at the skating rink who I was sure was the guy for me. He could skate backwards. Now if you ever had him ask you to skate, you knew you had arrived. One night it happened: he asked. I said yes, and I was right. I had arrived. You see, when he took my hands and turned around to skate backwards, I looked great. I couldn't skate backward to save my life, but while attached to him, I looked coordinated and graceful. The problem was I only went to the skating rink once a month with our church youth group. That didn't stop me from dreaming for hours about all of his wonderful qualities.

The next guy that I was sure was a keeper did not ride up on a horse or a pair of skates. He made his entrance into my life and my dreams on a surfboard. He came equipped with a good tan and shaggy blond hair. His boast was that he could teach me to surf in one day. I was going out to catch my first wave (it was a big one, I will admit) and the board got away from him. It caught me right in the stomach; and not only could I *not surf* after that one day's lesson … I couldn't walk. A bruise that wrapped around my entire waist was left to remind me of my shattered dreams.

As I look back at the men of my dreams at fifteen, I can easily see that they were one-dimensional. They each had one specific thing that drew me to them. However, the day came when they would get off of the horse and take off the hat, and the blue eyes looking up at me were two inches · below mine, making him five inches shorter than I had imagined. The skates and surfboards were gone and I saw them on the street or bagging groceries, and they were nice guys, but most of what I thought about them was made up in my own mind.

Somewhere between the age of fifteen and twenty-five, I had learned a few things about the choices I made and why. Thankfully, I had a highly developed system in place for making choices by the time I met my husband. I intended to see him as multidimensional. If we are honest, ladies, we all have our list of negotiable and non-negotiable qualities that we look for in a man. I felt like I found someone in Cam that surpassed all of my expectations. I loved discovering that I really preferred brown eyes, the kind that knew just how to look at me from under a hat. When Cam took my hand, I seemed to move alongside him effortlessly. Next to him, I always seemed to look better and more talented than I was. (Much better than I looked on roller skates.) Along with all these surprises, I found someone who was worth facing the big waves with, someone who would be with me until I was safely back on the beach. He was my dream come true. I could list, in some detail, why this was so.

I know at this point you are asking, "Why are you taking us through all of this?" I want to remind you, as well as myself, that we used to be good at this evaluation and list-making. In the Scripture passages that we visit today, we are going to be asked to do two things: *remember* and *return*. I hope you have already started some remembering of your own as you waded through my "blast from the past."

Bible Backup:

Song of Solomon (Song of Songs) Chapters 1 and 2

You can't read these chapters without seeing what God thinks about love. This earthly love between a husband and wife, a bride and bridegroom, tells another story as well: the story of the relationship God longs to have with us. God's word continually teaches us with pictures. If we get this earthly picture clear in our heads, it will help many other things make sense as well. God has always desired a relationship with His people. He wants to be clear about how He feels about us. This book of the Bible puts love into focus. Real love is always a pursuing love that asks the beloved to choose. Let's keep these principles in mind as we study Song of Solomon:

- God's word says that the marriage relationship is a pattern for discovering a relationship with Him.
- God's love, and the relationship He longs for, must be chosen, just as you chose your husband.

Read Song of Solomon Chapters 1 and 2.

Note: It is important to be able to identify *who is speaking* in these chapters, and to notice when the speaker *changes*. The masculine voice singular is the *beloved* (or *he*). The feminine voice singular is the young *Shulamite* woman (*she*). Additionally, the young woman will address the *daughters of Jerusalem (friends)*, and they will address her. If your Bible does not include headings showing the changes in speaker and audience, you may want to look at an online version of NIV or NKJ.

As you read, make *two lists*—one of words and phrases the Shulamite woman uses to describe the beloved, the other a list of the words and phrases the beloved uses to describe the young Shulamite woman. You aren't limited to Chapters 1 and 2. Take some time to skim through Chapter 5, where the young woman further describes her beloved, and Chapters 4 and 7, for more of the beloved's descriptions of the young woman.

Shulamite Bride's Words   The Beloved's Words

_____   _____

_____   _____

_____   _____

- The Young Woman's Descriptions of Her Beloved (Ch. 1, 2, 5)
- The Beloved's Descriptions of the Young Woman (Ch. 1, 2, 4, 7)

1. In verse 6 of Chapter 1, about which physical characteristic does the young woman seem apologetic and feel the need to give an explanation?

   _____

2. How does the beloved respond to this?

   _____

3. Did that exchange ring familiar to *you*? Is there something about yourself that you don't love but which your husband appreciates?_____

4. Now that you have these two lists, what do you notice about the *feelings* the lovers express for each other? If you had to summarize this for someone who has never read this book, what would you say?

   _____

   _____

   _____

5. Were you surprised to learn that most of the words or phrases used by the lovers describe _____ attributes?

6. What *clues* do the lovers in Song of Solomon give us about how to return to actually doing the things we first did when we were young newlyweds?

_____

7. Make a list describing the qualities you admired about your guy when you first got to know him:

_____

It's nice to know that listing the qualities of the one you love predates Elizabeth Barrett Browning's "How Do I Love Thee? Let me count the ways."

Read Song of Solomon Chapter 5

The saddest part of the story is told here in Chapter 5. He comes to her and asks her to let him in. He is drenched with dew from traveling to her in the night. Her response (verse 3) is that she's already taken off her robe and she would have to put it on again, and she has already washed her feet and they would get dirty if she walked to the door.

Has your marriage ever gotten to this point? Mine has. There used to be a time when my husband's arrival sent me running for the door. Sometimes, when he really needs me now, I say, "Really? I'm already in bed and I'd have to get a robe on, and I'll get my feet dirty running to the garage for you … just because the garage door opener doesn't work when you're on Big Red. Really?" I can even have this conversation with the luxury of a cell phone so I don't have to yell through the window.

There is a cure for the problem I have.

Jesus gives us His best advice for this in the book of Revelation. He says that if you have lost your first love, you need to *remember* the depths of that love and the height that you have fallen from it. Secondly, if you *return* to the things you used to do when that love was new, it will be rekindled. *Remember* and *return* are the words I hope will stick with us. Ladies, we need to start making those lists that we used to be so good at … the ones that list all of the reasons we fell in love with our husbands. As far as our actions are concerned, well, those may need to return to the responses that came so naturally to us in the beginning of our marriages.

I realize that marriage relationships can sometimes seem hopeless. It feels like there has already been too much brokenness to ever make everything right again. It is during these times that it is essential to follow our Lord Jesus's strong advice. It is the only plan I know that works. Do the things you felt like doing in the beginning, even if you don't feel like doing them now. Feelings will often follow actions.

Biblical Fact Check

We must first read the words as they are written to the church of Ephesus in the Book of Revelation. The Lord Himself is speaking:

> [2] I know your deeds, your hard work and your perseverance. I know that you cannot tolerate wicked people, that you have tested those who claim to be apostles but are not, and have found them false. 3 You have persevered and have endured hardships for my name, and have not grown weary.
>
> [4] Yet I hold this against you: You have forsaken the love you had at first. [5] Consider how far you have fallen! Repent and do the things you did at first. If

you do not repent, I will come to you and remove your lampstand from its place. (Revelation 2:2–5)

1. For what are they commended?_____

2. Are all of these good things?_____ Are they pivotal to the kingdom of Christ?_____

3. Of what are they accused? How serious is this, based on the warning given?

_____

4. Why is remembering essential for repentance?

_____

Now, let's look at the implication these words have for us as wives in our marriage relationships. Perhaps we could paraphrase these verses like this:

> Certainly, you have done well, working tirelessly in your home, caring for your family. You have persevered through hard times. You have been tenacious in guarding your home from evil, tireless in your church work, but you have left (or forgotten) your first love.

Jesus mentions another significant "R" word and that is *repent*. It is clear in our love story in Song of Songs that the bride repents about her response in Chapter 5. By the end of the chapter, she is making her lists again of all of the amazing qualities she still sees in her bridegroom. She sends him a sweet message that only He will understand. Read Song of Songs 2:5 and then read Song of Songs 5:8. She says the same thing in both verses. She repeats the phrase she said to him the first day she was in his arms: "I am faint with Love." In some translations it says, "I am Love sick." When she can't find him herself, she tells anyone who might see her bridegroom to tell him that she is faint with love. She needs him to know that she feels exactly the same way she did when their love was new.

Cam is the senior pastor and has a group of associate pastors that he works with at church. One day I saw a group of people enjoying themselves, laughing and chatting, and not wanting to miss out on anything, I joined the group. It was mostly our young staff, so I asked what was so funny. They told me they had just found this old picture of Cam and I had to see it. "Look at all of that hair ... look how skinny he is in this picture."

"What are you talking about?" I said "That picture is not that old. I think he still looks just like that." They looked at me like I was delusional (as only young people can do) and said, "No, he doesn't."

Their response cleared up the matter for me. This is what I learned while riding on my Big Red Harley. I'm the only one who can still see my bridegroom. I'm the only one who has the capacity to see him as he really is. The real man is *all that he was* mixed with *all that he has become*. I remember everything about choosing Cam for my husband thirty years ago. It gave me great hope that the flipside might be true as well. Maybe he looks at me and can still see his bride. It's more than enough for me if there is still one man who looks at me and sees that girl … and knows that girl … and still pursues that girl. There's nothing like it!

Personal Fact Check

- **Remember**: Have you made your list of all the reasons you fell in love with your man? Does it include those physical characteristics that you found so attractive when you first met?

39

- **Return**: What could you begin doing that you used to do when you first fell in love with your man? What do you think his reaction will be if you did this?

Group Discussion Questions:

1. Think of a time when you saw something familiar in a beautiful *new* way—perhaps from the perspective of your husband. Describe it.

2. When was the last time you looked at your husband in a new way or saw him in a new light? Where were you? What prompted this?

3. Does your husband have a "swagger" or some other identifiable characteristic that you find attractive? Explain. Does he know that you admire this about him?

4. How does it make you feel to think about him still seeing *you* as the girl who won his heart? Are you making it easy for him?

Recommended Reading: *When Sinners Say I Do: Discovering the Power of the Gospel for Marriage* by Dave Harvey

Biker's Trip Stats
&
Passenger's Log

*Starting/Ending Destination: Savannah, GA to Tybee Island, GA (25 miles)

*Best Highways to Ride: Highway 307 to 21N; right on Highway 30; left on Highway 25; right on Highway 17; take first exit after Talmadge Bridge; go through Savannah to East President Street

*Don't Miss This:

Houlihan Bridge (Highway 25)

Talmadge Bridge (Highway 17)

Savannah Wildlife Refuge

Tybee Island, GA

*Don't Miss This:

Lighthouse

Pier & Pavilion

Fort Pulaski

Tybee Island, GA ... home of the Tybee Island Pirate Festival and the Beach Bum Parade (biggest water gun fight in Georgia!)

We'll Be Back ...

AJ's Dockside Restaurant is a great spot for dinner at sunset, overlooking the river. We have been multiple times, and we will definitely be back again!

41

*Great Places to Eat:

The Breakfast Club

North Beach Grill (great place for a low country boil)

The Crab Shack

Sundae Cafe

Seaweed's

Delightful Detour(s):
Hardeeville, SC–US Wildlife Refuge
Hilton Head, SC

Cam Quote: "Every seat at the Northridge Cinema 10 is a recliner. There's nothing better than a good movie with your feet up!"

*Hilton Head Island, SC

Pinckney Island National Wildlife Refuge

Sea Shack (featured on *$40 a Day* with Rachael Ray)

Salty Dog Café

The Smokehouse (award-winning ribs)

One Hot Mama's Restaurant

Worth The Trip:
Lawton Stables is located at the Sea Pines Resort on Hilton Head Island. This is an unexpected treat for those who need a nature break. They have a small collection of animals that you can pet for free. And don't miss an opportunity to meet a horse named Harley.

CHAPTER THREE

The Harley Lean

"The more radical the road, the tighter you hold."

—Him

I will never forget my first lessons on *the lean*. Leaning is crucial in riding. I know to some of you this seems so basic it would not need to be discussed. However, for me, this was a foreign concept. Why would anyone want to tip that far over while going sixty-five miles an hour? It just didn't seem right. With my face moving closer and closer to the pavement, my brain was asking the only reasonable question: Is my husband crazy? As you might have guessed, I fought against that action. Thus my lessons in leaning went on for more than a day, with both Big Red and my husband extending me enormous patience.

Big Red is a big boy, as his name implies. If he were to go down (*tip over* doesn't seem to have the right respect), I was told that I would not be able to pick him up again by myself without further instruction. Tell me one more time why I would want to add my weight to the side that's heading straight for the pavement? Well, after countless explanations, some of the science made sense to me. The intricate physics, and the wrap-around armrests on my Harley seat, persuaded me to try this without the opposing action of leaning the wrong way. I know Big Red and my husband took it easy on me, but the end result was quite a ride. I think we even made it out of the neighborhood.

At one point my husband told me to stop thinking so much and just do what he was doing on each turn. "Whatever degree I lean, you lean, and keep looking in the direction we want to go." This was his nice way of saying, "Stop obsessing over the pavement." He told me, "When we're riding, you're never independent. You're always with me." Simple, right? Not so much. I have repeated that advice to myself many times to get me through the next turn. Very liberating. I didn't have to decide how far to lean—my husband did. I didn't have to decide when to straighten up—he did. I began to make a study (probably in an over-thinking kind of way) of the way his body moved and how to match my shoulders to his, even in the times I really felt we should pull up some.

Can you imagine a life where you aren't supposed to have an opinion about your husband's driving? I couldn't.

Surely he needed to know what I thought would be the best way to negotiate these curves. There is one problem with this logic. There's a *sound* a Harley makes that hampers good communication. I finally figured out, however, that this is part of the draw. Truth be told, limited verbal communication is on every husband's list for the making of a happy day. So I learned to save the really important comments for later. (We'll talk more about Harley-style communication in another chapter.)

As much as I fought against learning *the lean,* it was the one lesson I had to learn before I could experience the places I really wanted to go. You can't be in the Harley family long before you realize you have a list of places you *just have to* experience. There are highways in this great land of ours that *just have to* be driven and sights that *just have to* be seen from a motorcycle. One of these is the Blue Ridge Parkway and the surrounding area of Asheville, North Carolina. From my throne on the back of Big Red, I had an amazing view of those lush, green mountains. I was in wonder as ridge after ridge appeared around every curve. Each one was a different color green that shimmered under the sun or deepened beneath the shadow of the clouds. Sometimes the clouds were so low, they lay below the mountain ridges, gathering among the foothills and down in the valleys. After this trip, I was officially hooked on being a biker!

Okay, I'm not really a biker. I will always be the passenger. However, realizing I was now married to a biker, I did try to figure out what that made *me*. I don't think I've earned the *biker babe* role yet; I'm not hardcore enough, but I am sure I've reached *biker chick* status. After all, I do know *the wave* and *the lean*. So when people ask me, that is what I claim to be. It was this trip riding through the Great Smokey Mountain National Park that sealed my status in the eyes of my husband and the boys. I was doing a nice piece of leaning around those mountain curves.

Just in case I sound braver than I am, I have to admit that when the time came to conquer the famous Dragon's Tail on this particular ride, I found the best job for me was to stay at the cabin and have the steaks hot on the grill when Big Red and the boys returned. I haven't seen the Dragon's Tail at Deal's Gap up close and personal, but I have seen the pictures of my husband and Big Red in the lowest fathomable lean. It looked to me as if his left elbow and shoulder were feeling the friction of the pavement six inches below. If the stories around the table can be trusted, the number of adrenaline-producing hairpin turns can't be matched anywhere else. Three hundred and eighteen of them in eleven miles of highway to be exact! I was so glad to be on the welcoming committee and not on the road with them. After all, I've always believed some of the Harley time has to be just for the boys. I'm sure it's in the rule book somewhere.

I have been around many curves since those earliest lessons. I never seem to get past the point of needing to recall them. I realized it had been many years since I had worked that hard at being my husband's partner. If I didn't work *with* him, we wouldn't make the turn. Now, I admit Big Red handles nicely on the curves. The joy of the trip really rests on one variable: me. Am I with my husband or against him? He needs to know I'm with him at every turn.

The whole "learning to lean" thing boiled down to one word: *trust*. Not calling the shots, not making my own moves, but trusting someone else. Wait. I had to learn to trust all over again? How could this be? I thought I learned that trust thing years ago, back when I put my complete trust in my Lord, Jesus Christ. What strange creatures we are. We continually try to take back the control and demand to call all the shots. Now, when I'm on a particularly difficult strip of highway with some nice switchback curves, I just talk to the Lord and say, "This ride is just another lab for me to practice my trusting, right?" These lab tests, I realized, became the place I learned how to trust again. It was actually a sweet lesson, even if I still have to repeat the class from time to time.

As far as my husband is concerned, he likes a road with a lot of curves to navigate. "The more radical the road, the tighter you hold!" I guess I kind of like that part too. I really like the part where we are both looking in the direction we want to go … together.

Lessons Learned from the Back of a Harley

I was living in a marriage that I would consider close and connected. Cam and I could even teach very convincing classes in Marriage Seminars about staying close and connected. We would dedicate a portion of every Marriage Seminar to the topic of "creeping separateness," the drift that happens so gradually that you don't see it coming or know it when it has happened to you. Under these circumstances, I should have seen the distance between us, but I didn't.

When Harley rolled into our lives, I immediately noticed a few things about our marriage. I realized we lived in the same home, yet very independently of each other. I remember Cam and I shaking our heads at couples who had been married for a while, living with the attitude of, "I golf (add any word … fish, hunt, read), she shops (usually this word is the same), and we don't bother each other." We'd seen it a hundred times and firmly said that would never be us. The last thing we wanted was to wake up one morning and realize we were strangers. While I wouldn't say we were strangers, I knew we were living distanced lives.

Our Western culture honors independence above all else. Our culture, however, does not give the best advice on marriage. If you recall from Chapter One, we need to get our advice from the one who designed marriage in the first place. *God tells us that married people can become one.* This requires a give and take while continually considering the other person. The opposite of this is personal independence.

Cam and I have very independent personalities. We are strong leaders and thinkers, and we love that about each other. But the day we got married, I promised to consider his thoughts as important as my own. I believed in this kind of relationship with all of my heart. However, at this turn in the road, I saw a woman who had organized her world just the way she wanted it with little or no input from anyone else. I realized I didn't like this woman very much … and she was me.

I blame my job, really. (It must be something else at fault … it couldn't be me.) I was the Drama and Production Director at our church. At certain times of the year, I would be managing casts of hundreds and the surrounding production teams with scores of people. My main job description, as the director, in the final busy weeks of a production was trouble-shooting. I could fix things. I was good at it! All those teams had to do was listen to me—and, of course, do what I said. Have any of you ever made the mistake of taking your work home with you?

I don't think my family or my sweet husband ever officially used the term "control freak" in reference to me, but it might have passed through their minds. Something happens to you when that many people practice the art of doing what you say. When I was in director mode, we could enter a restaurant and I'd look around for what was wrong. Why do they have people waiting when those tables are empty? Or why did it take longer than the official sixty-second response time to get the waiter to that table and not this table? I was even heard saying, "I need to speak to someone about this. They'll be happy I told them so they can fix this." Cam would lovingly put his hand on my shoulder and pat it slowly, like you do for crazy people to calm them down, and say, "Honey, you are not in charge here." But I'm good at it!

When I choose to trust my husband and allow him to lead in our home, it is because I can feel the hand of my Savior patting my shoulder, saying, "Sarah, sweetheart, you are not in charge here." This reminder is life-giving to me, and healing to my marriage. Why? Because God planned it that way. It's not about who has the right plan and who knows how to fix things better. It's about learning to live in *dependence*.

I tell you all of this about me because I am often put in a different light than the one I just described. People assume I live in submission to my husband because I am weak or it is in my nature to follow. As a Christian wife, you may have people think this about you as well. I have had women say they won't go to a class I am teaching because I believe in that "submission stuff." What I wish I could shout from the rooftops is that the world completely misunderstands the teaching on submission in the Bible. Only the strong can submit. Anything else is subjugation. Jesus Himself shows us that the only way for submission to work is from a position of strength. You choose to place yourself under someone else's authority. Christ, in the same way, chose to put Himself under the authority of His Father, at every turn.

Bible Back Up:

The Book of Ephesians teaches us about the two words we need to remember this week: *love* and *respect*

Ephesians 5:21–33

Our Scripture stop this week is in one of the most famous passages in the Bible on the topic of marriage. As you process these verses, you may run across several words like *submission* and *head* that will not be popular. However, read the passage as a whole and listen to the phrases Paul uses to describe love. One thing will become clear: that kind of love means sacrifice.

Biblical Fact Check

Read Ephesians 5:15, 21–33:

> [15] Be very careful, then, how you live—not as unwise but as wise, [21] Submit to one another out of reverence for Christ. [22] Wives, submit yourselves to your own husbands as you do to the Lord. [23] For the husband is the head of the wife as Christ is the head of the church, his body, of which he is the Savior. [24] Now as the church submits to Christ, so also wives should submit to their husbands in everything. [25] Husbands, love your wives, just as Christ loved the church and gave himself up for her [26] to make her holy, cleansing her by the washing with water through the word, [27] and

53

to present her to himself as a radiant church, without stain or wrinkle or any other blemish, but holy and blameless. [28] In this same way, husbands ought to love their wives as their own bodies. He who loves his wife loves himself. [29] After all, no one ever hated their own body, but they feed and care for their body, just as Christ does the church— [30] for we are members of his body. [31] "For this reason a man will leave his father and mother and be united to his wife, and the two will become one flesh."[32] This is a profound mystery—but I am talking about Christ and the church. [33] However, each one of you also must love his wife as he loves himself, and the wife must respect her husband.

1. *In Genesis 2:24, God (the Designer) says that a man shall be united to his wife, and they shall become _____ _____. What do you think this means?*

2. *In the Ephesians scripture above Paul tells wives to _____ themselves to their own husbands. In order to submit to someone, you must first _____ them.*

3. *What is trust? How does it relate to control?*

4. *To enjoy the ride with Harley, in this chapter's story, I had to _____ to _____. Does this imply that the process of learning to lean could equate to the process of learning to trust? Could a Harley ride with my husband be a microcosm of my life with him?*

5. *God tells us exactly how we are to do this. He says we are to submit to our husbands the same way we submit unto the _____.*

Could it be that marriage is the laboratory in which we learn to live and trust our Lord? Is it possibly the place we practice relating to Him? (v. 32)

Love and *respect* are the tools God has laid out for you. Pick them up and start working on your marriage.

Love: Husbands are actually given the harder command— to live for your wife every day giving of yourself, like Jesus gave Himself for the church.

Respect: Wives, we are told to respect our husbands partly because God knew we wouldn't do that naturally. It won't just happen. We need to work at it.

I have a close friend who started her walk with the Lord a few years ago. She can clearly remember her life without the power of God present. She is on her second marriage to the same man, and her greatest desire is to have a different kind of marriage this time. She has been in several classes with me and will openly share her progress with the group at large. One day we were studying about honoring and respecting our husband. After she looked at what the Bible was telling her, she shrugged her shoulders and said, "I don't get it ... but I'll try it." Don't you love hanging out with new Christians? She took the Bible as if it were a prescription for her marriage and just tried it. Now the fascinating part of this story is her response the next few weeks. She came back all excited and said, "This stuff really works. I'm so happy, and my husband's happy. Mr. Wright really looooves me!" She is a very colorful character, and I can't tell you all of the other things she shared in class. Let's just say she always sparked up the conversation with her insights.

Why can't I respond to God's advice so quickly?

Look at the Bible and say, "This looks like good medicine. Why don't I take a dose for the good of my marriage?" When I realized that I had to learn to trust again, it was eye-opening. What was even more eye opening was the knowledge that when I trusted Cam, he felt respected. The one thing that God calls me to do as a wife was achieved by some good old-fashioned *trust.*

Trust equaled *respect* for Cam.

I trust you to make a good decision: about the next turn … or our future

I trust you to take care of me: on the bike … or in life

I trust you to lead: I see you as competent

I trust you enough to fit *everything I am to you*: I'll pull with you, not against you

I trust you even if it's scary: I'm in for the long hall

Trust helped me say the right things to Cam. One of those things was, "I respect you." One little hint from someone who has tried it: Respect works like magic on husbands.

They seem to flourish in an atmosphere of *respect* the same way we wives flourish in an atmosphere of *love*.

One of my favorite traditions that Cam and I honor and practice is having vision meetings. We plan these meetings twice a year: one in January to start the year off right, and one halfway through the year on our anniversary. We spend time getting on the same page about our home, children, grandchildren, ministry, and goals for the future. We talk honestly about where we have allowed a creeping separateness to invade our lives, and what it will take to get back to being united on any particular area. Cam calls me "a woman with an opinion on everything ... and not afraid to use it." He listens patiently to my opinions, and I listen carefully to his vision for the future. We have both figured out that our marriage only works right when we are both leaning the same way and looking in the same direction, focused on where we want to go.

Personal Fact Check

After spending some time studying the Word, I often take some time to journal my thoughts. The following three perspectives were ringing in my mind as I processed this trust issue in my life; spend some time journaling from these same perspectives. What might your husband say to you? What honest statement might you make to yourself? What do you think God is saying to you personally from His Word?

_____

_____

_____

Him:

"The more radical the road, the tighter you hold."

"When we're riding, you're never independent; you're always with me."

"Whatever degree I lean, you lean; and keep looking in the direction we want to go."

Me:

"It's the one lesson I had to learn in order to experience the places I wanted to go."

"The joy of the trip rests on one variable: me. Am I with him or against him?"

"This is just another lab test where I learn how to trust again, isn't it?"

"Only the strong can submit. You choose to place yourself under someone else's authority."

"When I trusted Cam, he felt respected."

God:

"Sarah, sweetheart, you're not in charge here."

To him: *"Love your wife."*

To me: *"Submit yourself to your own husband as unto the Lord."*

"Married people become one."

Group Discussion Questions:

1. "When we're riding, you're never independent. You're always with me." Rewrite this sentence in your husband's voice, filling in the blank with words that make this truth real for you. Don't stop coming up with words until you really get the point. "When we're _____, you're never independent. You're always with me."

2. What makes trusting such a hard lesson to learn? Why is it a struggle to trust?

3. "The opposite of relationship is independence." Do you agree with this? Explain.

4. Does "becoming one" mean that you lose all sense of yourself (your strengths, talents, gifts, personality) in the relationship? Explain.

5. Could the problem be prizing independence above oneness? (An older woman once counseled me, "Would you rather be right or be his sweetheart?")

6. Are you willing to buck our culture and do it God's way?

7. Do you really consider his thoughts as important as your own? Is this a choice you can make?

8. Read Ephesians 5:21–33. Why is the command for the husband the more difficult command? Do you think loving his wife sacrificially comes naturally to him? Why or why not?

9. Why do you think respecting our husbands doesn't come naturally for us? What keeps us from respecting them? (We think they doesn't deserve it? We think

we know more? We think we are more spiritual? We're waiting for them to do their part? We are proud? Etc.)

10. Would you like to be "leaning the same way and looking in the same direction" in your marriage? Is this a choice you can make?

11. Make your own list of statements that begin: I trust you to _____ (speaking to your husband). Perhaps you need to think back, remember times when he truly navigated the curves in your life. Try to remember how you leaned with him then. Now, watch for an opportunity to show him that you still respect him.

12. While it's true that the more radical the road, the tighter you hold, what does it cost your relationship when you forget to hold tight on the straight, unexciting, routine, everyday road?

Recommended Reading: *Love and Respect* by Emerson Eggerichs and *The Freedom of Self Forgetfulness: The Path to True Christian Joy* by Tim Keller

Biker's Trip Stats
&
Passenger's Log

*Starting/Ending Destination: Baneberry, TN to Fontana Dam, NC (109 Miles)

*Best Highways to Ride: 25 East; Highway 411; Highway 73 to Highway 129

*Don't Miss This:

Deal's Gap; The Tail of the Dragon (318 curves in 11 miles) [Highway 129]

The View of Douglas Lake [25 E]

Cam Quote: "There's two ways to experience Deal's Gap. The wise way allows you to run the Tail of the Dragon and get safely to the other side, turn left, and visit Fontana Dam. The foolish way allows you to contribute to the Tree of Shame (a giant tree fully decorated with wrecked motorcycle parts). But don't miss the experience!"

Newport, TN

*Great Places to Eat:

The Grease Rack (Great Steaks and atmosphere, in an old converted gas station–one of a kind)

Newport, TN ... home of the Harvest Street Festival!

Pigeon Forge, TN

*Don't Miss This:

Pigeon Forge, TN ... home of the Patriot Festival!

Dollywood Theme Park

Titanic Museum

The Dixie Stampede

The Comedy Barn

Smokey Mountain Harvest Festival

Smokey Mountain Knife Works

Catch it on the next trip: **Wheels Through Time** is a museum all about motorcycles. It's located in Maggie Valley, NC, which is a little out of the way, but it houses over three hundred rare motorcycles, so it will be worth the drive.

*Great Places to Eat:

Log Cabin Pancake House

Old Mill Restaurant (great southern cooking)

The Old Mill Pottery House Café and Grille

Alamo Steakhouse (won Best Steaks in the County for five years)

Bennett's Pit BBQ (voted Best BBQ and Best Ribs year after year; also recently voted Best Breakfast)

So We Hear ... **Applewood Farmhouse Restaurant** is in Sevierville, TN, which is just minutes from Pigeon Forge, TN. You will enjoy a great southern meal, which starts with their famous apple fritters. This place is surrounded with beautiful apple trees, so you will enjoy the view and the meal!

Fontana Dam, NC

*Don't Miss This:

Fontana Dam

> Fontana Dam, NC ... home of the Fontana Bluegrass Festival!

*Great Places to Eat:

Blue Waters Mountain Lodge in Robinsville, NC (beautiful views of Lake Santeetlah)

Delightful Detour(s):

Cherohala Skyway Loop (Highway 129; North Carolina 143/TN-165)
*Asheville, TN

*Asheville, NC

Blue Ridge Parkway

Biltmore Estates

Great Smoky Mountain National Park

> Worth the Trip ... It's worth a day out of your trip to take the Cherohala Skyway loop. The adventure will be in making time for the scenic lookouts and waterfall sightings. The ride is breathtaking!

CHAPTER FOUR

The Harley Gear

"It's every man for himself on this ride."

—Him

If you're going to walk the walk, talk the talk, and of course wave the wave, you have to give in to buying the gear. Before I was a biker chick, I thought that all of the black leather was just so you'd look cool enough to be accepted into the family. However, I found out that the black leather is just the beginning. There is a whole list of gear that is needed to survive on the road.

It's not that I was opposed to wearing something just to look cool. After all, when Big Red came to us, he was already geared up and looking good. He had enough silver studs on black leather just on my passenger seat alone to blind people when the sun hit just right. The last thing I wanted was to be an embarrassment to the noble throne. It didn't take me long to realize that there was another reason you needed to gear up on a Harley. Survival. Survival. Survival. A few cold rides with a wet patch thrown in here

66

and there, and I was more than ready to gear up. I let my husband know it was time to shop. I told him to buy me the jacket complete with chaps and boots. I had been ready for my boots since my first ride when I put my leg too close to the exhaust pipe.

We started finding the gear we needed anywhere we could—usually one item at a time with a good online deal—and I started to experience the difference that the right tools could make. Not only was the leather warm enough to see me through the coldest rides, but should I ever need it, it would also protect me better than anything else if we laid the bike down. I found all of this very informative and was glad to be on this learning curve. Some other useful information: the little dead bug bodies from the highway can't stain black leather. I became the proud owner of black leather chaps with braided leather down the side seam that matched my jacket perfectly. When worn with the boots, they made me walk like a cowgirl. I had to love that since I was born in Montana and raised in the west. I was getting back to my roots.

My husband was very helpful in teaching me about my gear: how to stow it and, most importantly, how to wear it. He patiently helped me get my chaps on right (which was no easy task) and checked how all of the pieces worked together. My man could regularly be seen checking my snaps or cuff zippers to locate those spots that only the wind could find. I was honored that he cared so much.

One fateful ride, however, all of this changed. It was to be our first group ride. We had ridden with other couples before, but we had never been a part of a large group. Imagine my surprise when he gruffly informed me, "It's going to be every man for himself on this ride, you know. If you want to wear your chaps, you need to learn how to put them on yourself." What? Was this the same man who had patiently cared for me on every other ride? Soooo, that's how it is, huh? Well, if that was the lay of the land, I'd show him. Who needed his help anyway?

I did!

It may sound easy, but putting on your own chaps is like learning to do everything upside down and backward. Maybe some people find it easy to get their eyes down level with their right rear hip, but I did not. Not only that, there was a problem once you did get down there: you needed one more hand (thus the need for your husband's help). Picture flinging a flap of black leather through your legs and catching it … your two hands holding it in place to thread an upside-down jacket zipper. You still need one more hand to actually zip it down three feet to your boots. This is crucial because failed attempts require you to remain in this side backbend pose long enough to get a cramp. The only remedy, really, is the side backbend to the other side to work it out. So, equal failure on both legs is required to be able to walk anytime soon. At this point, you haven't even thought about the giant snaps that await you down by your boots. I knew two things: the trip was coming and I needed practice.

Ride day arrived. The group was gathering in Fort Lauderdale. It was going to be a beautiful day in Florida. All was well. The sun was shining, and Miami was in our scopes. This was a great place for the girl who wasn't looking forward to putting on her own chaps. It was January, so even in the south it would be cold on the bikes once we got on the highway. So we started gearing up with jackets and gloves and decided that we could always stop if anything else was needed. I prayed the sun would just keep on shining so no chaps would be needed. We headed south on Highway 1 and intended to go all the way through the Florida Keys before it was all over. Our big goal for this ride was to be in Key West for sunset.

This still remains one of my most memorable rides. I can't explain why exactly. The culmination of this area's unique beauty, and the way it touches all of your other senses as well, makes it stick with you. As with most great Harley rides, the places you stop are as colorful as the scenery. We ate a basket of shrimp in a marina-side restaurant in Islamorada. These shrimp gave *fresh* new meaning. They tasted like they had been in the water minutes before gracing our basket. The lunch stop was just past Key Largo. After the good food and some crazy story-swapping (a requirement for each Harley stop), we headed down to a beautiful little place called Marathon where we would be staying for the night. We stopped long enough to check in, but after that we wouldn't stop again. It was Key West or bust.

The Keys amazed me! The broad expanse of never-ending sky and water seemed to wash all stress away. The beauty of the sun playing on the water changed its look with every hour. Seven Mile Bridge took us into a whole new world. On this day, with this ride, it was only right that our final destination was at the end of the world. Or so it seemed we had reached the end of the world. Do you know what is waiting for you at the end of the world? You guessed it—the Hogg's Breath Café. Anyone in the Harley family would be thrilled to find themselves at the Hogg's Breath, and I was no exception. I could tell Big Red thought he had come home.

We did it! Wow, was it worth achieving our goal! Sunset visits Key West with amazing regularity each evening. During its arrival, I felt a change in the air as all who witnessed it held a collective breath. The moment was honored by every living thing. What a remarkable event to be a part of. Every store emptied, and customers vacated their restaurant tables and wandered out into the evening. We were all magnetically drawn to the water to watch the sun make its regular descent into the ocean. Yet there was nothing regular about that sight. What an amazing artist our Lord is. To think, each evening He paints the sky with a new one. A sunset uniquely its own sizzled into the cool, glistening water. I was thankful to have seen it.

It had been a remarkable ride and a remarkable day. Yet my mind couldn't help but turn from the sublime to the ridiculous. I was still hoping I would not have to face the fateful *need-for-chaps* moment in front of *the group*. After the sun set, the temperature dropped enough to make it miserable on the back of Big Red. Everyone started gearing up … all the way up! I pulled in a deep breath and reminded myself that it was every man for himself and set about putting on my chaps unassisted. I worked quickly, trying to appear as if I'd done this a hundred times. I finished and turned around, proudly thinking everyone would care that I had achieved this in record time and with no help. As I surveyed the group, I saw the sweetest sight. A husband was lovingly zipping up his wife's chaps and checking the snaps near her boots, checking for just the right fit. All I could think was, "Wait a minute, didn't she get the memo?"

I almost mentioned to my husband that I guess she didn't get the "every man for himself" talk. But thankfully, I kept my mouth shut and just gave him the upraised eyebrows instead, which I'm sure he knew meant he would hear about it later. With a little lopsided grin, he asked, "Can I help you with that?"

He started lovingly tucking my scarf around my neck so the wind wouldn't get in, and I lovingly replied, "No, that's all right. I've got it! It's every man for himself. Remember?" So we rode off into the Florida moonlight for the long trek home.

I wasn't many miles down the road before I was thinking of the hundreds of little ways my husband had checked on me and worried about my comfort and safety. I realized that night my Harley man is a little like his Harley. When they are all geared up, they seem pretty loud and grumbly on the outside ... but inside they're teddy bears.

My southern gentleman husband returned by the time we rode the next morning, and all grumbling was gone. I was grateful to be heading into the Everglades with all of his protective instincts going full force. Alligator Alley was one place I didn't particularly want to stop. I held on tight as we had dozens of gator sightings. I enjoyed the view at sixty-five miles per hour. No need to slow down on my account.

We have learned to laugh about the chaps talk. I still like to bring up the story about the godly husband who served his wife so lovingly in front of the group. Cam still holds to his position, the view that it's got to be every man for himself so no one holds up the group. Most of the time now if we're gearing up, I'll hear him grumble, "Get over here ... let me get that zipper." Then there's his gruff, "Put your boot up here and let me check those snaps." I love the way he cares!

Lessons Learned from the Back of a Harley

The big lesson I am continually learning on the back of Big Red is to see myself clearly. When I do, I am usually able to see Cam in a different light as well. This "every man for himself" lesson was one of the big ones.

Every time I look at Cam through my judgmental eyes, he looks worse than he is. I blame colorful expectations and a grand view of what I hope our marriage can be—and he blames hormones. Whatever *it* is that causes me to see him through this lens, it colors my view of him. My judgmental thoughts sound something like, "I can't believe you treated me like that! I would never treat you in that way." During the cold ride home from Key West, my busy little mind was saying, "I would never ..." and the Lord tapped me on the shoulder and said, "Really? Never?"

I may never have told him those words, but I had given him the message with my actions. There were two areas in my life that pushed my husband out of his number one spot ... that place where he could count on daily care from me: our children and our ministry. Both of these changed our pace of life. *In short, busyness forced us to live differently as a couple.* Can anyone else relate?

The change happened when our children were born, and it lasted until they left our nest. Let's give me some credit for initially staying balanced. Child number two really started to tip the balance in our home. We were told that number one would change everything, but he seemed to go wherever we went and do whatever we did. When our second son came along, I expected life would function the same as it always had, but I was surprised to find I couldn't even get to church on time. When our third son came along (yes, we had a son every two years like clockwork), I realized I didn't have enough hands to even go to the mall. The exact state of my life became evident when, in June, my oldest asked as we entered the mall if we were going to see Rudolf. I hadn't even darkened the door of the mall in six months. *It was during this phase that I basically informed Cam that it was every man for himself ...* even if I didn't say the words.

I had my hands full. My phone calls to Cam were usually something like, "The older two just put the baby out of the window ... I know it's only a three-foot drop ... no, he's not hurt ... yes, he liked it ... but what if he got away before I could get out the front door?" When he would come home midday, our conversations sounded something like, "There are Cheerio bowls on the floor because they were puppies today and no amount of coaxing would convince them to eat at the table like little boys. Did you want them to starve? If you don't understand this, I can't explain any further." *I basically informed Cam that he had no idea what my life was like, and I didn't have time to figure out what his life was like.* (Not in so many words, however.) Busyness. Can anyone relate?

The ministry stress on our marriage didn't hit like a ton of bricks the way parenting did. It was a gradual pull. Church work looked very much like a group motorcycle ride. There was a big group of people who needed to be considered and cared for. The group sometimes had to take precedence over the one. The *one* in this case was each other. The *one* I had promised to "love and cherish … til death." *Why do we push those closest to us back on our consideration list?*

The daily love and care for our spouses seem like the little things in marriage. *They are, however, the really big things.* It is in these little actions and considerations that we best show our spouses *love* and *respect*. Let's not forget that *love* and *respect* are our calling as wives and husbands. Do you know what your spouse's love language is? There is a great book by Gary Chapman called The Five Love

Languages that teaches couples to find their love languages and to speak them. This book could be a great tool for you as a couple. The best teaching from this book, in my view, is to not assume that your spouse speaks the same love language you do.

I believe you and I probably already know our spouse's love language without the help of a book. I say this because when we get mad at them, we refuse to speak it. May I suggest that you try and put into words the things that really make your spouse feel loved and respected? There may be five basic love languages, according to the Smalley study, but your spouse is a unique blend that only you can discover. Let's get honest about what we already know says *love* to our spouse. The next step is to figure out what you don't know and become a student of this person you are married to. Finally, you need to learn to speak this language fluently. As with all valuable pursuits in life, this will take some practice.

Bible Backup:

Proverbs 31:10–31

We have to visit this passage during this lesson because the Proverbs woman is the ultimate busy woman, and what's worse is that she is the ultimate perfect wife. In Scripture headings, she may be called the *virtuous* or *worthy woman*, but I have come to call her the *perfect wife*. Read verses 10 through 12 with me: "An excellent wife, who can find? For her worth is far above jewels. The heart of her husband trusts in her, and he will have no lack of gain. She does him good and not evil all the days of her life."

Does that mean *every* day? Who is this woman? I've been studying her for a while now, and you will notice that after these three verses singing her praise, there are sixteen verses that list all that she *does*. Don't read them … they will make you tired. Then we get to verse 29: "*Many daughters have done nobly, but you excel them all.*" This is her husband speaking at this point. Again I say, "Who is this woman?"

I found out! You'll be happy to know that she doesn't exist. She is actually a composite of the best advice a mother could give to her son, the king. I get this now. I raised three sons. If I was going to describe a woman worthy of them, it would be quite a list. That's just how we mothers of sons are. This still didn't let me off the hook. In the first part of the chapter, this wise mother is warning her son of the dangers that will ruin his life and his kingdom. In that warning, one of the big dangers listed, is connecting to the wrong kind of woman. Then, more than half of her advice is about marrying the right woman. She tells him in beautiful language how valuable a good wife will be.

Biblical Fact Check

[10]A wife of noble character who can find? She is worth far more than rubies. [11] Her husband has full confidence in her and lacks nothing of value. [12] She brings him good, not harm, all the days of her life.

[13] She selects wool and flax and works with eager hands. [14] She is like the merchant ships, bringing her food from afar. [15] She gets up while it is still night; she provides food for her family and portions for her female servants.

[16] She considers a field and buys it; out of her earnings she plants a vineyard. [17] She sets about her work vigorously; her arms are strong for her tasks. [18] She sees that her trading is profitable, and her lamp does not go out at night. [19] In her hand she holds the

distaff and grasps the spindle with her fingers.[20] She opens her arms to the poor and extends her hands to the needy.[21] When it snows, she has no fear for her household; for all of them are clothed in scarlet.[22] She makes coverings for her bed; she is clothed in fine linen and purple.[23] Her husband is respected at the city gate, where he takes his seat among the elders of the land.[24] She makes linen garments and sells them, and supplies the merchants with sashes.[25] She is clothed with strength and dignity; she can laugh at the days to come.[26] She speaks with wisdom, and faithful instruction is on her tongue.[27] She watches over the affairs of her household and does not eat the bread of idleness.[28] Her children arise and call her blessed; her husband also, and he praises her:[29] "Many women do noble things, but you surpass them all."[30] Charm is deceptive, and beauty is fleeting; but a woman who fears the LORD is to be praised.[31] Honor her for all that her hands have done, and let her works bring her praise at the city gate. (Proverbs 31:10–31)

Focus on the verses that speak to the husband/wife relationship:

1. *"The heart of her husband _____ in her..."* *(Proverbs 31:11 NAS "The heart of her husband trusts in her, and he will have no lack of gain.").* *What does this mean? Does he know that you've got his back, or is it every man for himself in your marriage?*

2. *"She brings him _____ and not _____ all the days of her life" (v. 12). Jot down a few ways you could do your husband evil.*

3. *"Her husband is known in the gates, when he sits among the leaders in the land" (v. 23). In what ways might your husband be known in the gates in your particular life circumstances?*

4. *"She speaks with wisdom" (v. 26). Are your words wise or wounding? Do you reflect an attitude of kindness toward your husband, even in your seemingly insignificant day-to-day remarks?*

5. *List the blessings that the virtuous wife herself receives when she accomplishes these things. (You*

should be able to find one in each of the following verses: 10, 17, 18, 20, 21, 25, 28.)

I think God wants us to know this woman because no matter how busy she was, she didn't forget that the little things are the big things when it comes to her husband. No matter how many other people there are to take care of outside her home *"she looks well to the ways of her household"* (verse 27). She does good to him *every* day

Are there some days I imply, "You're on your own. We can't impede the progress of this busy family machine or church machine or work machine" or "Fend for yourself. You're a big boy"? Is this the language I'm speaking, or do I choose to speak the language of love, his personal love language? How can my husband's heart trust in me if he's not sure which language I'll be speaking?

Personal Fact Check

Review Lesson: Remember! You can only fix yourself.

Let's be honest … practical steps to begin the fix.

- *Remember what you know: God wants you to show love and respect to your husband.*

- *It's the little everyday responses that show whether you really love and respect him.*

- *And (here's the biggie—look at yourself clearly) you already know what your husband's love language is. When you're mad at him, you refuse to speak it.*

Take a few moments to journal your thoughts about seeing yourself clearly. What is the Lord showing you about *you*? If you don't know, pray that He will show you something that you need to be honest about. He probably will.

_____

_____

_____

Group Discussion Questions:

1. Have you ever experienced a sight so magnificent that surely every living thing who witnessed it would pay homage to the Creator who made it? Describe the sight.

2. Were you ever dressed up (geared up, uniformed up) for an event (or task, or job), and worried that

you might be exposed as a rookie, or worse yet, incompetent? Explain.

3. When was the last time you were grumbling about something your husband had done (or not done) and the Lord softened your heart by reminding you what a sweet guy you married? List a couple of sweet things that you remembered about your guy on that occasion.

4. What story have you and your husband learned to laugh about over time?

5. Make a short list of the ways your husband shows that he cares.

6. Can you identify with the idea of pushing your husband into the background when your children came into your lives? What did you stop doing for your husband that was once a priority?

7. What about work? Has that become a priority over your husband? Is there anything you could change to fix this? Do a bit of problem solving, as if this were a work assignment.

8. Think of how *you* respond to small, daily acts of care and affection. How do these make you feel as a woman and a partner? Now put yourself in his place.

9. What simple things do you do daily to show your guy how important he is? Make a list. Is your list shorter than it was in the beginning of your relationship? Have your actions become conditional?

Recommended Reading: *The Excellent Wife* by Martha Peace and *The Exemplary Husband* by Stuart Scott and John MacArthur

Biker's Trip Stats
&
Passenger's Log

*Starting/Ending Destination: Fort Lauderdale, FL
to Key West, FL (188 miles; be there by sunset)

*Best Highways to Ride: A1A;
Florida State Road 934; US 1

Fort Lauderdale, FL

*Don't Miss This:

Fort Lauderdale, FL ... home of the
Fort Lauderdale International Film
Festival!

Bonnet House (old homestead with gardens and monkeys)

Miami, FL

*Don't Miss This:

Miami, FL ... home of the Miami River
Day Festival!

Miami Drawbridge (US 1/SE 2nd Ave)

*Great Places to Eat:

The Big Pink

The Rusty Pelican (on the water)

Cam Quote: "You know it's
a great stay when you can
watch the sun set on one
balcony and the sun rise on
another."

Marathon, FL

***Don't Miss This:**

The sweeping views from the Seven Mile Bridge

> Cam Quote: "So, I hear you can dive for spiny lobsters in six feet of water. We'll be back." (As long as you're not within three hundred feet of the shoreline.)

Key West, FL

Don't Miss This:

> Key West, FL ... home of the Pirates in Paradise Festival!

Dry Tortuga National Park

Harry S. Truman Little White House

Ernest Hemingway Home and Museum

We'll Be Back ...

Famous for its live entertainment and good times, the Hog's Breath Saloon offers live music and great food. Cam was heard saying he's "got to have that pulled pork sandwich one more time."

***Great Places to Eat:**

Hog's Breath Saloon

> Cam Quote: "Alligator Alley provides the best motivation for staying out of the ditches that we've ever run across. A line of alligators stand guard on both sides of the road."

Delightful Detour(s):
Airboat ride on Alligator Alley
Everglades

> Worth the Trip ... (After the sunset, of course) just to put your feet in the clear, warm, 70 degree water at Higg's Beach in January. The memory keeps you warm through the long, cold *night ride* back.

CHAPTER FIVE

Harley-Style Communication

"I have to get off this bike, and I mean now!"
—Me

I heard *the call*. I can't believe I'm saying this, but I really heard the *Harley Call*. My husband would often tell me that he had heard *the call*. "Need to go ... Big Red is calling."

I would smile and respond with, "Yeah right," and then secretly wonder if I should start worrying that he now communicated with Big Red on that level. But then it happened to me. Big Red was calling, and I *had* to go.

We were in Steamboat, Colorado. The sun was shining, and there were blue skies as far as the eye could see. Not simply blue, but that special kind of blue that is reserved for the tops of mountains on a summer day. I've always wanted to capture that blue and bring it inside for my walls or wear it around my neck as a scarf. But it is only for mountaintops and can't be captured. From our stationary vantage point, the mountains were breathtaking. I could have been content to sit on the porch all day. But then I heard it—*the call*. Big

Red was beckoning. It was time ... we had to conquer that next mountain.

I shouldn't have been surprised that my husband had heard it as well and was already packing up for the day's adventure. Our first stop was to be Estes Park, Colorado. This ride would take us through the Rocky Mountain National Park. We would cross the Continental Divide and be at the very top of the mountain on Trail Ridge Road. We would be above the tree line, with wide-open expanses surrounding us. I had been there before, but I had not seen it from the back of a Harley. I had learned by this time that the best way to see the Rockies is from the back of Big Red, a fact my brother and husband both tried to tell me years ago. They loved hearing, "You were right," coming freely out of my mouth. (They never expected that to happen.)

We headed out, leaving the beautiful Steamboat Mountain and Chisholm Trail, with its grassy summer ski slopes, and headed to that next mountain we needed to conquer. We faced this warm, cloudless July day with great anticipation. Our highway followed the river, with its wonderful, winding curves, and the sights around each bend in the road made me giddy. (Giddy is not usually how I like to describe myself, but it seems other words fall short of capturing the feeling of the moment.) Catching a glimpse of the sparkling sun-kissed river against the dark green mountain, with its chiseled peaks, took my breath away.

Part of the way into the trip, when the climb and the turns started getting intense, we spotted our first signs of a weather change. We were going around some hairpin turns that were putting my leaning skills to the test. Let's just say it was no longer the beauty taking my breath away. I had inhaled so many times without exhaling, I had stopped breathing altogether. Then the rain came, followed by sleet and snow, which in turn was followed by hailstones. Add to the not breathing, the fact that I could no longer move. I felt like I was frozen solid. Not breathing … not moving … I was having trouble letting my driver know that I needed to stop. I started with one small finger tap. This would never do! I woke one arm up and let the pounding begin. He thought I was giving him a shoulder massage to get his circulation going.

When we finally found a spot to pull over safely, I was more than a little curious as to why it took so long to stop. I was promised that if I ever needed to pull over, we would pull over. He had several reasons why he didn't, one being he thought I would rather get through it as fast as we could.

I, on the other hand, had passed my limit. I wasn't going to make it one more minute! We needed to improve our communication!

Taking a break for a few minutes helped. Any time without the wind cutting through to our bones was a blessing. We bundled up with everything we had on the bike, which wasn't much, and continued down the other side of the mountain to Estes Park. We rode in cold, driving rain the rest of the trip. Estes Park was not supposed to be our final destination, but I was thinking it would have to be my final stop. I was making a plan while we rode. My first order of business was to be some honest communication.

When we stopped in a parking area under the first cover we'd had in hours, I was thankful just to be alive. We were taking inventory of all moving body parts at that point. My husband had that look in his eyes that said, "You are some kind of woman." We made it through rain, sleet, snow, and hail, not to mention the plummeting temperatures throughout the day. I was glad he was proud of me, and I would probably ride through that kind of weather again sometime. *But not today!* was all I could think. I told him that Estes Park was a nice town and I had decided to stay right there. After all, they had stores and a cute café that specialized in hot tea, and I had a book. I think it's important to know when you just can't go on, and I was there. Then a miracle happened. My husband said something he never says: "You're right. I think you should shop."

Suddenly my energy came back. My limbs were warming up. My eyes were sparkling again, but all I could say was, "Really?" I told him to go on down the other side of the mountain and finish the ride that he had planned. I would be fine for hours now that I could enjoy a nice cup of hot tea followed by some accessory therapy.

My husband and Big Red conquered the rest of the mountain and finished their ride to Longmont, Colorado. While they were there, my husband went shopping too! I couldn't believe it. He picked out matching rain outfits for us from the Harley store. These suits were worth their weight in gold. When worn over all of our other layers, they kept the wind and rain at bay. I shared my joy in knowing that my husband liked shopping too. I was immediately corrected. You might need this information as I did. Bikers don't shop; they "gear up," and whatever you do, don't call what they bought "matching outfits."

For those of us who are not too proud to be caught shopping, let me give some advice. When on a Harley, accessory shopping is best. This would be handbags, scarves, and jewelry. This is important because you can still do some serious shopping and carry it home on the bike. For all other treasures found, there are three little words to learn: "Ship it, please." My great finds of the day were a handmade shoulder bag and some uniquely designed jewelry. With my shopping treasures stowed with the rest of the gear and my rain suit on, we headed back over the top of the mountain to get home to Steamboat. I had plenty of time to keep working on my new communication plan that was so needed.

Communication on Big Red had always been a mixture of vocal messages and our form of sign language. I think I mentioned earlier that we didn't make it as easy as buying headsets for our helmets. We were purists and preferred hollering and gesturing to get our message across while we rode. On a normal day riding, my husband could hear me pretty well (hollering in his ear leaning over his shoulder), but I couldn't hear him. This was due to the way the wind hit the back seat. It was a strange turn around for our marriage because I usually heard everything. I often warned all of my family that I had dog ears and to be careful what they said. Add a little driving rain and hail hitting my helmet, and I couldn't hear a word.

The new plan was genius—simple, clear, and to the point. My husband would love it. I realized that with our tapping communication that three taps already meant very positive things, such as, I love you … I saw that … I'm all right … it's all good. Three taps for three syllables. I knew we couldn't change the positive sign because three taps or pats had meant I love you for a long time now. The crisis tap was the one we had to work on. I fell back on our old lifeguard training and realized that the strong two taps meant you were in trouble. We would both relate to that. So I started a list of word phrases that two taps could mean: stop now … slow down … watch out … I'm cold. It had to work better than the continual tapping I had done on his shoulders on the way up the mountain. Those taps represented a nonstop flow of syllables. (Or maybe just eleven syllables: I need to get off this bike, and I mean now!)

At this point I know you are starting to worry about me and wonder if I'm crazy. (They say high altitudes can have that effect.) You're wondering who would put that much thought into inventing a whole new communication system:

a woman desperate for good, clear communication. That's who. A woman who desires to hear and be heard. That's the lesson I learned on the back of a Harley. I am that woman. Clear communication takes work.

Lessons Learned on the Back of a Harley

In Chapter Four, we talked about learning the love language that our spouse speaks. It is important to differentiate between that language and verbal communication. Love languages may have nothing to do with words at all. They are probably best spoken with our actions—the loving and caring that we live out for our spouse, rather than the words we speak and the messages that we send with our mouths.

Let's talk communication. You don't have to be in a marriage more than a week to know that communication is going to be an issue. It takes you that long to figure it out, because up until the *week* point, you are blinded to all issues in your marriage. You still believe that there couldn't possibly be issues in your marriage. The good news for all of us is that we are not alone. Every marriage has to deal with communication-related difficulties. The reason for this is because two people who speak different languages got married. *The way men communicate and the way women communicate are entirely different.* If you see people who look like they have this part of their marriage under control, it is because they have worked at it. It doesn't come naturally.

Cam and I started working at this communication thing almost immediately. There is research on just how differently men and women communicate. After trying to process this research and going through our own trial and error in our marriage, the best advice we could give as we taught marriage seminars was to look at the person you married and say, "You speak a different language than I do." This helps only because you now know you will need an interpreter or you will need to learn the language yourself. This keeps us from falling into what I refer to as the "meatloaf trap." In the first months of our marriage, Cam said to me, "I meant to tell you, I really don't like meatloaf." What I heard was, "I really don't like any of the food you make." I think most of the communication problems happen not because of what is said, but because of bad interpretation of what was said.

Interpreting what our spouse says is what fuels the myriad of conversations that take place with our girlfriends over lunch, ladies. "Can you believe he said that?" accounts for probably 90 percent of my lunchtime counseling chats with married women. Obviously, both people trying to accurately interpret one another *is* the best-case scenario. It's always fun watching couples figure this out in the early years of marriage. Our oldest son, Cam IV, came to share some recent enlightenment with us. It became apparent that he and his wife, Hailey, could say the same exact phrase and mean entirely different things. He was shocked to find out that when they said, "We need to get this done," he meant yes, we need to get this done this week some time. He shared in some confusion, "Mom, when Hailey says we need to get this done, she means by five o'clock today." You gotta love a man learning to interpret his wife accurately.

I love the fact that Cam boldly encourages the men of our church to work on communicating with their wives. "Trust me on this as your pastor," he tells them. "I promise you can learn to do this well. It doesn't happen on its own; it takes work. It's just like swinging a golf club. You can learn how to do it if you want to." You would be surprised by the number of men who take this challenge seriously. Ladies, we seem to communicate with ease, so again, we don't think we are the ones with any work to do. As I said before, this book isn't about fixing anyone but ourselves.

Let's ask ourselves a few questions. **What are the communication traps we women fall into? How can we avoid them?**

Say what you mean clearly: avoid the "beating around the bush" trap

If you ever see a man with his palms out, pleading, "What did I say? What's the matter? What did I do?" please take pity on him and realize, he really *doesn't* know what's wrong or what he did to offend you. We are usually very helpful with our reply of, "Well, if you don't know, I'm not going to ____ ____!" Every woman can fill in those two small blanks. For the men reading this book, the blanks are "tell" and "you." What is needed here is a little honesty. "When you did this I felt____. When you said this I heard____. Is that what you meant to say?" Any of these responses allow for a more accurate interpretation. Cam tried to teach me early on in our marriage that the worst way to communicate with him was through hints. I now believe him, and have proof of my own, that he doesn't get hints. It doesn't mean he doesn't care.

Don't over talk the situation: avoid the nagging trap

Statistics tell us that women will usually speak about twice as many words in a day as men do. Even being married to a professional talker, I can attest to the fact that by the time he is with me in the evenings, my husband has used up most of his words. Knowing that he isn't going to be talking much, I usually just start filling space with my voice. I usually cover the topic from several angles until Cam says, "I got that the first time." I've tried to convince him that I'm not nagging. I was just not sure if he heard me, so I repeated myself. Cam has a good ear and a bad ear. It has something to do with shooting when he was young, so he's had this impediment for years. The boys will often ask me, "Which is Dad's bad ear?"

I have to reply, "The one I'm speaking into." Let's be honest, sometimes our men practice selective listening. One solution for this is for women to avoid falling into the Nagging Trap. I think the only fair compromise is for men to try and listen longer than they naturally want to. And women, save a few of your words and call a friend. (Yes, he has informed me it's not nice to make fun of a person's impediment.)

Guard the climate of your home: Avoid the Belittling and Bossing Trap

It was a good day when I figured out that I controlled the climate of our home with my communication style. When this became clear to me, I banished the things that poisoned the atmosphere. Belittling comments were the first to go. (The bad ear comment not included.) I know my man better than anyone else, which means I see flaws no one else sees. (He sees mine as well.) Dwelling on these does not warm up the climate in our home. It is impossible to live in a state where you never measure up. Ladies, if we continually try to fix what we see wrong in our husbands, what they hear from us is, "You aren't quite there yet. You're not enough." What other interpretation could there be? With belittling comments comes the temptation to become verbally bossy. You are not your husband's mother or his boss. Do you really want to be either of those? Don't let your communication style send the wrong message. I wanted the climate in our home to be one my husband could thrive in. To quote my friend Renee, "He faces fixing what's wrong at work all day long. There should be one safe place where he is free from that."

Every marriage has to deal with areas that need fixing. May I encourage you to set healthy boundaries when doing this? Set a time and place away from your private, intimate space to discuss your hard issues. Get some help to communicate. Home, however, will be a very cold place if it is always about fixing the other person.

Bible Backup:

The ageless teaching in the Book of Proverbs gives us the best comparison between wisdom and foolishness. This biblical material is unique because it works even if you are not a believer. With the New Testament teaching, we are clearly taught that the life Jesus offers can only be lived by the power of the Spirit. If anyone tries to live the Christian life without Christ, they find very quickly that it is impossible. Anyone, however, can read Proverbs and improve their life by following the instructions for the wise man or woman. It is simply true. It's like gravity. You don't have to believe in gravity for it to happen in your life. It just happens. One of the main truths taught, however, is that the wise man will choose God.

Clearly my marriage needs the power of Christ to survive the battering of the world. What my marriage also needs is some good Old Testament wisdom—reminders of what is *just true,* taught to me by the One who made all things. Let's look at some of His wisdom.

Read these verses from Proverbs and keep them in mind as you go through the Biblical Fact Check:

"The wise woman builds her house, but with her own hands the foolish one tears hers down" (Proverbs 14:1).

"A wife of noble character is her husband's crown, but a disgraceful wife is like decay in his bones" (Proverbs 12:4).

"He who finds a wife finds what is good and receives favor from the Lord. The role of wife was always intended to be a blessing" (Proverbs 18:22).

"Better to live in the desert than with a quarrelsome and ill tempered wife" (Proverbs 21:19).

"Better to live on a corner of the roof than share a house with a quarrelsome wife" (Proverbs 25:24).

"A quarrelsome wife is like a constant dripping on a rainy day" (Proverbs 27:15).

The one thing that can turn us from a blessing to a burden, ladies, seems to be our mouths. Is it possible that we could be tearing down our own house with careless, negative speech? There is wisdom in working on what we say and how we say it. Communication skills are well worth the work they take to acquire.

Biblical Fact Check

Proverbs 14:1

1. The _____ woman _____ her house.

2. What does the Lord say the foolish woman uses to tear her house down? What does this imply about my blaming the destruction of my family on someone else?

Proverbs 12:4

1. A wife of _____ character is her husband's _____.

2. Think about the word *noble*. What does it mean to you? Does your definition include words like *honesty, strength, respect,* and *fairness*?

3. Now, consider the word *crown*. What picture does it paint in your mind? Can you see how a wife's noble character brings honor to her husband?

4. A disgraceful wife is like _____ in his _____.

5. Food For Thought: Bone marrow is the source of healthy cells that heal and repair the body. Decay implies that something toxic or poisonous has set in. When the Lord says the disgraceful wife is like decay in a man's bones, what is He saying about the *seriousness* of having a wife who is not of noble character?

Proverbs 18:22

1. He who finds a wife finds that is _____ and receives _____ from the Lord.

2. Think of the Creator, the One who designed marriage to be the ultimate expression of love. Imagine His total delight in looking down upon you and your husband and thinking in His heart, *That's my girl! My man found good.* List the ways you, as a wife, are good for your husband.

Proverbs 21:19; Proverbs 25:24; Proverbs 27:15

1. What word is used to describe the wife in all three of these verses? Use a dictionary to find the definition of this word. Copy a few of the synonyms too. Do you want these words to describe you?

2. In each of these verses, the husband appears to be seeking _____.

I heard Dr. Laura Schlessinger being interviewed at a conference I was attending. The book she was talking about was her latest book at the time, entitled *The Proper Care and Feeding of Husbands.* I was so fascinated by what she said that I stood in a long line to get my book signed. I guess I was hoping for a few more drops of insight if I saw her up close and personal. She has written many books and has been on a radio talk show for years. Her work has helped many couples save their marriages, and I wanted to find out how. I was surprised to find that what she teaches isn't exactly rocket science, but it is full of wisdom. She asks wives to do simple, positive things to honor their husbands. One assignment she gave was for wives to think of three compliments to tell their husbands every day for a week.

In one week, there were reports of changed marriages. *Something so simple made a difference!*

I was very humbled by reading her book. She doesn't take it easy on us women. But like the bride in Song of Solomon, we should always be able to list our husband's good qualities. Why do I fail to compliment and encourage with disciplined regularity? It is evident from Proverbs that our mouths are very powerful. They can build our house up or tear it down. Do whatever it takes to learn how to have positive communication in your home. Invent a whole new sign language if that is what it takes for understanding to reign in your home.

Personal Fact Check

- Journal: Which of the communication traps discussed in the lesson are most problematic for you? List them in their order of prominence in your relationship. Reflect on this list. Be honest with the Lord as you journal about what's number one on your list. Describe yourself as your husband may see you.

_____

_____

_____

- Choose at least four of these Proverbs verses from the lesson to *memorize* (the ones that speak loudest to you): Proverbs 14:1; 12:4; 18:22; 21:19; 25:24; 27:15. Ask the Lord to bring these to your mind before you get careless with your words.

Group Discussion Questions:

1. Remember a time when your husband gave you a look that said, "You're some kind of woman." Where were you? What was the situation? How did that look make you feel?

2. Think of a humorous example of miscommunication in your relationship, like my pounding Cam on the back to get him to stop and he thinks it's a back massage.

3. Do you have a secret, nonverbal communication that means "I love you"?

4. What is your crisis tap or look? Try to describe it.

5. In what way (and in what area of your lives) have you communicated to your husband that he is not enough?

6. Reflect honestly on the ways you may have "torn down your house with your own hands" (Proverbs 14:1). How could you set about to repair this?

7. Would "She is a Blessing!" be the first words to come out of your husband's mouth if he were asked to describe you? If not, what do you think his first words would be?

8. What do you think about Dr. Laura's assignment— coming up with three compliments a day, for a week? In what areas could you compliment and encourage your husband (his physique, beautiful eyes or smile, strength, compassion, steadiness, tenacity, work skills, intelligence, commitment to you and the family, kindness, generosity, gentleness, sense of humor, etc.)? Are you willing to commit to doing this regularly?

Recommended Reading: *The 5 Love Languages* by Gary D. Chapman and *The Proper Care and Feeding of Husbands* by Dr. Laura Schlessinger

Biker's Trip Stats
&
Passenger's Log

*Starting/Ending Destination: Steamboat Springs, CO to Boulder, CO (176 Miles)

*Best Highways to Ride: US 40; US 34 (road may be seasonally closed), which turns into US 36; CO 66/US 36N; CO 66/CO 7/US 36E; CO 7/US 36 E

Steamboat Springs, CO

*Don't Miss This:

Strawberry Park Natural Hot Springs

Steamboat Springs, CO ... home of the Annual Hot Air Balloon Festival!

*Great Places to Eat:

Winona's

The Egg and I

Saketumi Sushi

Cam Quote: "Great breakfast ... worth eating any time of day."

Hot Sulphur Springs, CO

*Don't Miss This:

Hot Sulphur Springs Resort & Spa

Hot Sulphur Springs, CO ... home of the famous hot sulphur springs!

*Great Places to Eat:

Glory Hole–great breakfast

County Seat Grill and Pub

Granby, CO

*Great Places to Eat:

Granby, CO ... home of the Fly Fishing Festival and the Festival of Trees!

Maverick's Grille

Ian's Mountain Bakery & Pizzeria (home of the famous Wake and Bake Cheesecake)

Grand Lake, CO

*Great Places to Eat:

Grand Lake, CO ... home of the Pelican Festival and Parade!

Sagebrush BBQ & Grill (great western atmosphere)

Estes Park, CO

*Don't Miss This:

Stanley Hotel–visited by many of the rich and famous, including Stephen King. This hotel was the inspiration for his book *The Shining*. The hotel was also used for some of the filming of the mini-series of *The Shining*.

Cowpoke Corner Corral–horseback riding

Rooftop Rodeo (usually in July)

Elk Fest (October)

So we hear ... DeLeo's Park Theatre Café & Deli was featured on Food Network's *The Best Of* for their sandwich, The Big Reuboni.

*Great Places to Eat:

Mountain Home Café Inc.

(great breakfast)

Rocky Mountain National Park

Rocky Mountain National Park ... home of the Scandinavian Midsummer Festival!

Moraine Park (great place to see wildlife)

Horseshoe Park (great place to see wildlife)

Trail Ridge Road offers eleven miles of highway travel above the tree line for stunning views!

Continental Divide Trail

Estes Park, CO ... home of the Annual Wool Festival!

Boulder, CO

*Don't Miss This:

Chautauqua Park

Cam Quote: "Trail Ridge Road is the only place in America I know where you can ride in 50 degree weather and sleet in July!"

Flagstaff Mountain (great views)

Boulder Creek Path

*Great Places to Eat:

Foolish Craig's Café (featured on Food Network's *Diners, Drive-ins & Dives*)

Zolo Grill

The Pinyon

Lucile's (great breakfast, but must be willing to wait)

Delightful Detours:

Timnath-Wellington–Clark Reservoir
Fort Collins–Horsetooth Reservior

Worth the Trip ...

See the ranches nestled in between the mountain ridges as you ride the back road from Clark Lake. What a place to build your life. It's hard work, but just think of what you get to look at every morning.

CHAPTER SIX

Harley-Style Contentment

"Those seals must not need much."

—Me

What do we really need to survive? Food, clothing, shelter—is there anything else? I could think of one thing: a way to see my grandchildren. As a new grandparent, I was sure I couldn't survive without that luxury. Learning to simplify would be our goal for a month. I suggested we try it for a shorter period of time, but Big Red convinced us to try it Harley-style and go for the whole hog. We jumped in with both feet clad in black leather Harley boots: a month minus all of the trappings we were used to, such as comfortable shoes and my favorite blanket. Downsizing everything would be required.

Let the packing begin … or should I say unpacking!

Everything I put in the duffle bag was met with the inevitable words, "You think you're really going to need that?" Now this was not just any duffle we were packing; it was an airtight waterproof duffle not unlike the ones used by Navy Seals. In fact, it was precisely the same bag. From my husband's perspective, a prestigious tool of this nature should not be filled with the mundane or frivolous. This was never going to work. Could our marriage survive this paring all the way down to survival-level existence? To be honest, I knew it would survive, but something had to give. Just when I was trying to figure out what or who that was going to be, my husband showed up with—you guessed it—my own personal duffle bag.

We would have a basecamp to come and go from, but all traveling needs had to fit on the back of Big Red. I use the word *basecamp* in the broad sense just to give you a picture of the nature of this month. If you pictured a very rustic survival place in the northwest mountains, let me focus that picture for you. We would be living in a cute one-room loft apartment with a tiny kitchen and bathroom surrounded by a beautiful garden with a good reading bench. Making it sound like I'd be living in a tent for a month is not fair to you girls who can really pull that off. I could at least see the hiking trails from my bench, but most important, they didn't lead to any outdoor bathrooms. Thankfully, I had one of those inside.

Space negotiations were tedious, as we did not see eye-to-eye on the worth of certain items. For example, a quart of oil for Big Red verses the need for both shampoo *and* conditioner for me did not hold equal weight in my husband's eyes. Big Red won out again when it came to a coveted spot in the side compartment that was perfect for a hair dryer … but for some reason a tool bag claimed the spot. My husband was showing favoritism, and Big Red was winning. Guidelines were set up that stipulated that we each had to fit all of our personal needs into our own Navy Seal duffle. (Those Seals must not need much.)

I finished the final packing and unpacking that was required to meet the stringent "need" prerequisite of each item with agonizing care. I was extremely proud that the normal twelve bottles of face and hair products from my bathroom had been downsized to five, and that was only one of my victories. However, when I arrived for the big load up, my husband looked anything but proud of me. Even after I shared my huge win with the bottle victory, his eyes kept returning to the load in my arms and the things hanging from each shoulder. Handing over my duffle, I explained that the other item was an overnight bag that I never travel without, and then there was the last, not-so-explainable bag that I was calling my purse. Inside were my purse and several other critical items I couldn't live without. Hoping he would be as understanding as the airline personnel, I smiled and said, "See, just two carry-ons, and if I forgot anything, I'm sure there is a store there."

Without a smile in return, he loaded Big Red. I guess in his mind he pictured two sleek black bags latched behind Big Red as we sailed down the highway unencumbered. I really didn't think the four extra orange Bungee cords, needed to strap down the added bags, were that distracting from the original vision. We may have looked slightly top heavy. Let's just say our luggage was now at a good height to be a head rest for me. With a promise from me to leave most of it at the basecamp during the rest of our trips, we were off.

We were on the road! Joy had returned to our little family. It may have taken us a little longer to pack than our other trips, but I was sure it would be worth it. *Let the adventures begin!*

We would be traveling all around the northwest United States, with most of our time in Washington State. Why? To stay within driving distance of my grandchildren, of course. Having spent a lot of time in the mountains of Montana and Colorado, I thought I would feel like I was seeing the familiar. I found once again that I was experiencing the completely unique work of the Master. Our Lord, in His creativity, never seems to make a duplicate mountain. We would go the scenic route by way of Idaho and the top of Oregon before we arrived in Washington. We would see Mount Hood and eventually be back to the place where Mount Rainer reigns above all the rest. We were familiar with this mountain. We knew that being in close proximity to it alone would have been interesting for a month. Bathed in a blanket of clouds, with one massive peak rising above— or shown in full view on a clear day—Mount Rainer is worth the trip. Did I mention that the best view of the mountains is from the back of a Harley? It would never do for me to get promoted to the driver's seat—I'd have to watch the road too much.

But watch the road I did! I was mesmerized by it. We had hugged family good-bye in Somers, Montana, and headed out across the northwest corner of this beautiful country of ours. I felt a kindred spirit with the earlier explorers of this vast land. I wondered what treasures we might find along the way. I wondered if they too had trouble packing only the necessities. I wondered many times who in the world thought that it would be possible to tame this land with roads. I spent my time not just road-watching, but mountain-, river-, and valley-watching as well. It was fascinating.

That treasure we found turned out to be the Columbia River Gorge. Maybe a better way to describe it would be as the motherlode of treasures all bundled together with the shiny ribbon of the gorge. It was during this leg of our journey that I realized that there was too much grandeur to just see and forget. I needed to start logging this beauty and listing places to come back to. After all, like the explorers who had gone before us, we had a responsibility to report back to others about travel conditions and food availability. So at our next stop, I made some notes about the things we had seen and some really good pie.

As we neared our destination of Seattle, Washington, the mountain terrain started meshing with a new water culture that we would grow to love with a passion during this month-long venture. Those welcoming views are still some of our favorites today. Our basecamp was on Bainbridge Island, so Big Red was about to experience his first water travel. I was a little apprehensive about the ferry ride on a motorcycle, but I think he kind of liked it because motorcycles have a place of honor on ferryboats. We crossed the beautiful Puget Sound with the best seat in the house and found out on the other side that motorcycles are also the first off a ferry. My husband and Big Red both looked thrilled. Life doesn't get much better than that.

We were off to make ourselves a little home for a month!

The ground rules were set. Willingness to be spontaneous on any day that called for a road trip was at the top of the list. A day to rest your saddle-sore body was perfectly acceptable as well. A little reading each day with your boots off and your feet up was a prerequisite. It sounded like the perfect life to me.

Every time I sighed and said, "This is the life!" I turned around the next moment and said, "This isn't working. I need to fix this." By day two, I was fretting over not being able to make a good cup of coffee. By day three, I was worried about the internet not being very reliable. By day four, I was complaining about every day being a bad hair day, with the ever-present helmet hair and the never-present equipment needed to fix it. I can't even mention the tiny, minute issue that had me frustrated on day five. I was definitely learning some lessons about myself.

As the month ended, this is how I would describe my process toward contentment.

Week One: I was *obsessing* over what I wished I had brought from home.

I had just the right equipment at home to make the perfect cup of coffee and fix the hair issues.

Week Two: I was *busy* working on getting what I wanted another way.

I realized regular trips to Starbucks would handle both the internet and coffee issues.

Week Three: I was *intrigued* by how little I needed and even more intrigued by how very little I wanted in my possession and under my control.

The pleasant, unexpected perfect cup of coffee made just for you by someone else brought such joy. The face-to-face conversation that *just happened* with precious family and friends instead of the unsteady FaceTime that I was sure I couldn't live without.

Week Four: I was *content* and actually *dreading* returning to a life with so much stuff to manage.

I spent time thinking about how to go home and not get encumbered with unimportant stuff.

As I look back, I seem to have a long list of joyful memories that filled our days: The best lunch spot found in a tiny town beside a tiny post office with a picnic table in the backyard to eat our homemade sandwiches. The best view of a mountain harbor from the highway and bridge coming into Poulsbo, Washington.

This Viking city was settled by Norwegian people because it reminded them of their homeland. I had the joy of feeling at home in a strange place surrounded by people I didn't know because I too came from similar roots. Also I feel I should report that the town had some good ice cream.

The best destination was a ride out to the longest spit of land in America, near Dungeness. I didn't even know land masses had spits. The best afternoon was spent in the company of retired movie animals at the animal park, laughing uncontrollably. There was one old ex-performing bear that you would have thought was stuffed, he moved so little and expended so little energy. However, when a roll was thrown his way, he whipped one paw up so fast, it was a blur. He caught the roll every time, but his arm was the only part of his body to move. What a place to retire.

A walk in a wooded park with children and grandchildren ended in the best picnic ever on a driftwood beach looking across the water to Mount Rainer. Hours of talking about very important stuff, like how God sanded that wood smooth for us to enjoy, and how He put it on the beach, was definitely on my list of bests. The best rainy afternoon was spent in a quaint, tiny theater, feeling cozy with my guy as we shared popcorn. And last but not least, the best place to get that perfect cup of coffee made by the people who really know how to make it and roast it, Storyville Coffee.

I have to report that my biker chick skills continue to rise. I can gear up quickly and pack for a day trip in the blink of an eye. I can chat with other bikers about that "bad bike" they are riding and mean it. I rarely wish I had brought anything else with me. All in all, my contentment level while on the back of a Harley is pretty high because I've figured out what is essential. It is also due to the fact that I have conquered helmet head and bad hair days with just the right pair of sunglasses or the perfect scarf to put on at restaurant or shopping stops. Don't confuse these with the hardcore glasses I wear with my helmet. These were purchased with only fashion in mind. Both of these items pack easily into my allotted space so other people are content as well.

Lessons Learned from the Back of a Harley

When I looked back at the month of Harley travel, I saw a microcosm of our marriage. Figuring out the phases I went through to gain contentment opened my eyes. I couldn't help but see times when I lived in those same phases during our marriage. Most of the time it was never for just a week.

Let's look at the first two. Most of my marriage struggles happen when I choose to live here.

Phase One: I was obsessing over what I wished I had

Often as women, we have a set picture in our minds of what our homes and our marriages should look like. We spend quite a bit of time forming these pictures until they are perfect. We believe contentment will come when reality reaches this standard. When reality falls short of this picture, we obsess about what we don't have. In short, we waste energy on what we don't have and forget to see what we do have. Let me give you an example concerning "things." I have no memories of lusting after any woman's husband, but her couch was a different story. In fact, while I'm confessing, I remember several women and several couches that haunted my dreams for a perfect living room. The living room in my mental picture was stealing my daily contentment. Sadly when I lived those days grumbling about the state of my couch and a houseful of boys who could destroy it, my heart had no room for thankfulness about the fact that I had three healthy boys with couch-destroying energy.

It becomes even more dangerous when it is not about things. We start comparisons about what other people have as relationship realities. We tell ourselves things like, "She has a husband who has more time for her … her husband talks to her more … he interacts with the kids more." As soon as we tell ourselves any of these poisoning messages, our contentment will flee because our marriage is falling short of our perfect picture. Comparison is deadly to our marriage. We will revisit this in our Bible time this week. God's wisdom concerning this starts way back with the Ten Commandments.

Phase Two: I was busy getting what I wanted

In answer to discontentment in our marriages, we proceed to figure out ways to grab what we want. In our culture, this sounds like a noble response to our issues. *It's all on me, and I'm going to handle it.* The problem with this is that you are in a divine relationship (with God) and a divinely designed relationship (with your husband) that this culture cannot understand. Strangely enough, you will find true contentment when you trust your God for your needs, and when you partner with your husband instead of working in opposition to him.

Cam and I have enjoyed teaching marriage conferences together in every season of our ministry. It seemed like every time we were preparing for one of these retreats or conferences, however, we started seeing some issues raise their ugly heads in our marriage. So we were always promptly reminded that we did not have all of the answers. We figured out, after watching this pattern, that we need to address several topics regularly in our marriage classes. Cam would always tell newlywed couples, "I don't know when your first fight will be, but I can tell you what it's going to be over: money." For some reason, money issues have a way of controlling more of our marriage contentment levels than they should. We have had to fall back on a practice that we started as a young married couple. We look at each other and admit we need to pull together on this, whether it's a couch or college tuition. Then we start a process of looking at our life filtered through this one question: Is it a want or a need? This same question comes back to my mind, whether I am struggling to be content for a month or a lifetime. It's a simple system. We work hard and trust God to supply all of our needs. We as a couple agree on the *wants* and partner together to plan and save for them. When I was young, I thought it would be a good plan for God to just dump money down from heaven so I wouldn't have to worry about it and I would be content. I could serve Him wholeheartedly because I wouldn't be worried about money. Now I realize that I wouldn't have this whole list of ways that He met our every need in the nick of time. This is the list that reminds my heart to be thankful. As far as the blessings we have because we worked together as husband and wife, those things have cemented us together as nothing else.

I pray that I will choose to live today within these last two phases. I'm sure I will have some discontent in my tomorrows, but I know I can choose another way. Let's briefly unpack these options.

Phase Three: I was intrigued

Phase Four: I was content

I was intrigued by the discovery of what I didn't need. I experienced a divine curiosity about where my contentment really comes from. I pursued this divine curiosity daily to see how God would "work all things together for good" in my marriage. I had to settle my part however by choosing a thankful, trusting heart.

Take a moment to journal about a time you found Him faithful. What are the things that keep us from trusting Him?

Bible Backup:

Comparisons are deadly for your marriage. God makes this pretty clear as He warns about the sins that will ravage your life. Let's go all the way back to the part of Scripture known as the law. Moses describes the reason for God giving these words to His people like this: "Keep His decrees and commands which I am giving you today, so that it may go well with you and your children after you and that you may live long in the land" (Deut. 4:40). Moses does not say they were given so that God would have a punishment system. God's law, given to His people after they came out of a life of slavery, is the most beautiful group of life-lessons and warnings ever compiled. They were given in order to save His children from pain and give them a bright future. Let's just look at the basic outline of God's desire for His people, the Ten Commandments. All of the rest of the Law fits within this outline. The first part deals with how we should relate to our God, and the second part is how we should relate to other people. This would encompass every other relationship we have and most definitely touches on our marriage relationship.

Read Deuteronomy 5:21:

> "You shall not covet your neighbor's wife. You shall not set your desire on your neighbor's house or land, his male or female servant, his ox or donkey, or anything that belongs to your neighbor."

Comparing our marriages to others is just the first dangerous step. It will, however, lead to sin—the sin God calls coveting. He knows the toll this will take on your marriage. God's goal is not punishment but protection.

Divine curiosity may help you see life return to your marriage. Let's move to the New Testament for the rest of our biblical help. We are not left with a list of things to just try and do and hope it helps. Whether Old Testament or New, we are reminded that if we want the other relationships of our life to go well, we need to consider God's thoughts. He tells us that worry is not the answer.

> [25] "Therefore I tell you, do not worry about your life, what you will eat or drink; or about your body, what you will wear. Is not life more than food, and the body more than clothes? [26] Look at the birds of the air; they do not sow or reap or store away in barns, and yet your heavenly Father feeds them. Are you not much more valuable than they? [27] Can any one of you by worrying add a single hour to your life?
>
> [28] "And why do you worry about clothes? See how the flowers of the field grow. They do not labor or

spin. ²⁹ Yet I tell you that not even Solomon in all his splendor was dressed like one of these. ³⁰ If that is how God clothes the grass of the field, which is here today and tomorrow is thrown into the fire, will he not much more clothe you—you of little faith? ³¹ So do not worry, saying, 'What shall we eat?' or 'What shall we drink?' or 'What shall we wear?' ³² For the pagans run after all these things, and your heavenly Father knows that you need them. ³³ But seek first his kingdom and his righteousness, and all these things will be given to you as well. ³⁴ Therefore do not worry about tomorrow, for tomorrow will worry about itself. Each day has enough trouble of its own. (Matthew 6:25–34)

Underline the word *worry* in the scripture above. If you had to put it in one sentence, what would you say is the best way to get what you want?

_____

_____

Do you believe God has designed marriage? Do you believe He knows how it works best? Do you believe He wants the best for your marriage? Are the desires of your heart safe with Him? Write a short prayer in answer to these questions.

_____

_____

_____

> [7] "Ask and it will be given to you; seek and you will find; knock and the door will be opened to you. [8] For everyone who asks receives; the one who seeks finds; and to the one who knocks, the door will be opened.
>
> [9] "Which of you, if your son asks for bread, will give him a stone? [10] Or if he asks for a fish, will give him a snake? [11] If you, then, though you are evil, know how to give good gifts to your children, how much more will your Father in heaven give good gifts to those who ask him! (Matthew 7:7–11)

Underline the word *ask* every time it is used in the scripture above and circle the word *give* every time you see it.

Your marriage should be something you consistently cover in prayer. Start journaling some specific prayers you are praying for your marriage. I believe marriage is one of the good gifts God gives us. I don't think we have been left on our own to figure it out. Let's continue to ask the master designer of this relationship for His wisdom. Make it a habit to write down your requests regularly, and be ready to write down the good gifts that show up in your marriage.

In short, worry is not the answer; prayer is!

Is it possible that contentment may come first in your relationship with God and secondly in your marriage?

_____

_____

_____

Biblical Fact Check

Write Deuteronomy 5:21 in modern language. What might all of those warnings be concerning in your marriage?

_____

_____

_____

Jesus had a way of taking an Old Testament law and packing it with a New Testament heart response. For example, He would say something like, "You have heard it said do not commit adultery, but I say don't even lust in your heart." There is the letter of the law and the spirit of the law, and Jesus always goes for the spirit. With the Deuteronomy 5:21 spirit, He might be saying to us, "You have heard it said, 'Don't covet,' but I say, 'Don't even compare.'"

Their marriage looks easy. She has help cleaning her house. *Jesus answers, "Don't compare."*

We'd be happy too if we had all that stuff. *Jesus answers, "Don't compare."*

I wouldn't ever worry if my husband had that job. *Jesus answers, "Don't compare."*

Comparing will lead to anger, blame, and coveting. These sins will eat at the contentment in your marriage. The funny thing about it is that you started comparing because of your desire for contentment. Thank the Lord for His warning and don't travel down that road.

The New Testament verse in our study this week may take us down a better road toward contentment. Look at these verses again and journal any new thoughts you have about contentment.

Matt. 6:25–34

_____

_____

Matt 7:7–11

_____

_____

Personal Fact Check

In each chapter, at this personal fact check stop, our goal is to discover something new about ourselves. I hope during this particular exercise, you and your spouse will work together to discover something about you as individuals and as a couple. When you do, you will inevitably find out some things that you need to know about your marriage. (We don't usually give the husbands homework, so ask nicely, girls.)

I speak with confidence on this topic because every time Cam and I have done this exercise, we have had our eyes opened to something new. We call it the Pyramid of Priorities. Great thinkers have been using the pyramid to chart learning concepts for all different topics for thousands of years. Cam got excited about some things he had learned about leadership from Coach John Wooden when we first got married. Because of that, he thought we should use a pyramid. As we were talking through some issues one day, he suggested we chart them. We used the pyramid like this: Choose eight different priorities you have set for your marriage and place them on the bottom level of the pyramid. If two had to go away, decide what two you would give up first. Take those away, and write the remaining six on the next rung up on the pyramid. This is repeated until you get all the way to your top two priorities and you have to decide between the two.

The brilliant part of this exercise is that each rung represents thoughtful conversation between the two of you. Getting the first eight priorities settled is, in and of itself, a great conversation. Listening to the other person's side and why things are important to them is eye-opening. For example, if one of your marriage priorities is both of you working in the field you were trained in, and another one is the desire to have a parent be the main caregiver for preschool children, there may come a rung at which you have to decide which one you'd give up first. This is a healthy thing to discuss and hear the other person's heart on, but it is a lousy thing to fight over continually because you don't know where each of you stands. The point is that you hear each other out and decide together which things move up a rung. This makes you face issues before they get to a crisis level and every conversation turns emotional instead of thoughtful.

Try it out. Fill out the pyramid below:

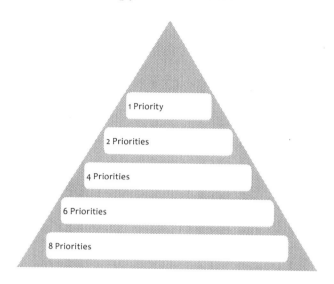

The pyramid of priorities is a way for you and your spouse to settle some of the big issues in your marriage. Strangely enough, it works on small issues as well. Cam and I had several of these conversations about *wants* and *needs* and where they fit into our priorities in order to plan this month-long trip. We have often used this to have family meetings with our children on goals for a year. Conversation was heard about family trips, mission trips, sports involvement, time with friends, time with God, and the list goes on. The point is that everyone was heard, and we all had to agree it was a priority for us as a family.

It's just a tool. I realize as you read about this pyramid chart, that it doesn't sound like that much fun to live through the process of using it. I know that, because as I reread this section, I get the same impression. Can I just say that in real life, these are some of the most amazing conversations that I remember having? Even the ones that weren't that fun to have left an open window for me to look through into the heart of this person I love.

Group Discussion Questions:

1. Can you identify with the phases I experienced in my search for contentment in my marriage? Share an example from your own life of *Phase One: Obsessing* and *Phase Two: Busy Getting*.

2. Have you ever had the opportunity to experience *Phase Three: Being Intrigued* by what God might have for you and your marriage? Where were you? What was the situation? How did God speak to you? What did you learn?

3. What do you think is the biggest thing holding you back from *Phase Four: Contentment* right now in

your marriage? A needs list that is too big for God, an unwillingness to forgive someone for something, a distance that has developed in your relationship with your husband, your own insecurities, fear of the future, a too-small view of God, a reluctance to trust Him because you don't know Him well enough? Based on the scriptures in this lesson, where could you start?

Recommended Reading: *The Marriage Builder* by Dr. Larry Crabb

Biker's Trip Stats
&
Passenger's Log

*Ride 1: Starting/Ending Destination: Somers, MT to Seattle, WA, by way of Columbia River Gorge and Mount Hood (791 miles)

*Ride 2: Starting/Ending Destination: Seattle, WA to Sequim, WA (67.2 Miles)

*Ride 1: Best Highways to Ride: US 93; I-90; US 395; I-84; OR 35; US 26; I-84; I-405; I-5

*Ride 2: Best Highways to Ride: WA-305N; WA-3N; WA-104; US-101N

Somers, MT

> Somers, MT ... Home of crystal-clear Flathead Lake: the largest freshwater lake west of the Mississippi River in the contiguous United States.

Coeur d'Alene, ID

*Great Places to Eat

> Coeur d'Alene, ID ... Home of the famous floating green

Capone's Pub (featured on *Diners Drive-ins and Dives*)

Jimmy's Down the Street Cafe (featured on *Diners, Drive-ins and Dives*)

Cafe Carambola

Wolf Lodge Inn Restaurant

Columbia River Gorge

*Don't Miss This:

Lower Oneonta Falls

Columbia Gorge Sternwheeler Dining
and Sightseeing Cruises

Multnomah Falls (breathtaking views)

Kayaking

Fishing

Windsurfing

> Cam Quote: Wolf Lodge Inn Restaurant–When several southern men ride to a meal ... a cow must die!

We'll Be Back ...

The Lewis & Clark Highway is the beautiful, scenic drive on the other side of the Columbia River Gorge. If you time it right, you can stop in Stevenson, WA, for the Bluegrass Festival.

*Great Places to Eat:

Solstice Wood Fire Cafe (Hood River, OR)

3 Rivers Grill (great lunch place–Hood River, OR)

Mount Hood

*Don't Miss This:

> **Mount Hood** ... Home of the Huckleberry Festival and Barlow Trail Days

Huckleberry Festival and Barlow Trail Days

Salmon, Mushroom, and Bigfoot Festival

Bonneville Dam

Windsurfing

Kiteboarding

*Great Places to Eat:

Rendezvous Grill

Dragonfly Cafe and Bakery (Brightwood)

Ivy Bear Pizzeria (Aldercreek)

> Catch it on the next trip: Troutdale, Oregon, is a hundred-year-old town in the Mount Hood area that we will be sure to visit next time to experience its charming main street antique shops and general store.

Portland, OR

Beautiful City Parks

> Portland, OR ... Home of the Waterfront Blues Festival

Seattle, WA

*Don't Miss This:

Pike Place Market

The Space Needle

> Seattle, WA ... Home of Seafare Seattle, named one of the top ten events in the country

*Great Places to Eat:

Ray's Boathouse

Chandlers

Anthony's

Red Mill Burgers

> Mount Rainier: tallest peak in the Cascade Range
>
> Lake Washington: largest lake in King County
>
> 520 Bridge: best view of Mount Rainier
>
> Lake Union: best place to view sea planes taking off and landing

Bainbridge Island, WA

*Don't Miss This:

Faye Bainbridge State Park (great view of Puget Sound)

Fort Ward State Park (best driftwood collection)

Harvest Fair (October)

First Friday Arts Walk (every first Friday of the month)

*Great Places to Eat:

Rolling Bay Café

Blackbird Bakery

Big Star Diner (featured on Food Network's, *Diners, Drive-ins and Dives*)

Poulsbo, WA

Poulsbo, WA ... home of the Viking Fest

*Great Places to Eat:

Mora Iced Creamery

Azteca Mexican Restaurant

Cam Quote: Azteca Mexican Restaurant ... the Molcajete is to kill for! Maybe not kill ... but begging would be appropriate.

Worth the Trip ... Storyville Roasting Studio is a beautiful, picturesque place to sip the most amazing cup of coffee or espresso. It's located on Bainbridge Island, just a short ferry ride from Seattle.

CHAPTER SEVEN

Harley-Style Celebration

"Let's celebrate!"

-Me

"Exactly what I was thinking."

-Him

"Let's celebrate!" I said, the day our month was up. It had been thirty days in our cute little room with the tiny bathroom, tiny kitchen, and little bed with the close quarters I'd learned to love. Those close quarters had been even closer on some days with the drop-in visits from friends or family, and I had loved every minute of it!

The day had come, however, when I was ready for a little change of pace. The first words out of my mouth that morning were, "Let's celebrate," to which my husband replied, "Exactly what I was thinking." Now when I mentally previewed the way this conversation might go, I had hoped to hear something quite close to his response, but maybe with a little something added, like, "Whatever you want, my love. What do you want to do?" As it stood, however, I knew I had better figure out exactly what he was thinking.

We knew our next stop was Canada and that we were ready for some wide-open spaces. The problem was that qualifications like "some good food and room to eat it in" looked like a big steak at a roadside biker dive on the plains of Canada to him. I was picturing a big king-size bed with feather pillows and someone handing me tea in a china cup overlooking a rose garden at the Empress Hotel. I had obviously already googled Victoria Island, Canada, at this point. Let the negotiations begin.

Celebration ideas temporarily tabled, we headed out on our next adventure. Our route through Sequim to Port Angelo took us past glorious sights of America's purple mountain's majesty that perfectly framed the fields of lavender. We inched our way across the vast Olympic Peninsula, and I tried to log the view around each curve in my memory as a snapshot to be looked back at with joy. When we reached the point where land and water collide and shades of silver and deep blue fought for the eye's attention, I thought, *This is celebrating!* The trip ahead was exciting to me no matter the outcome. We were leaving the country, and traveling over land and sea. Another ferry ride greeted us as we crossed into Canada. Big Red handled ferry rides better than I did, so I walked on the ferry as he and my husband navigated the steep ramp that led to the belly of the boat. Already this country was different than ours. Where was Big Red's place of honor he usually enjoyed on Seattle ferries?

Our next stop has now turned into something we laugh about often. However, on this particular day, we learned when to stop laughing. This might be the time to give you a deeper glimpse into my husband's personality. He is fun-loving and gregarious. He loves to laugh, and the only thing he enjoys more than laughing is making other people laugh. Anyone who talks to him for five minutes feels like he is their best friend. He can often be heard introducing perfect strangers to each other. As a new guy walks up, he'll say, "Have you met my friend John?" and these two strangers will start a friendship. Now let me be perfectly clear: there is nothing fake about this. My husband and John both believe they are good friends, and if they spend any longer in conversation, they will seal the deal and remember each other for a lifetime. Oh, to have such people skills. If only they had worked on this particular day.

We arrived at the border-crossing gate where the border patrol, comprised of Canadian Mounties, had everything well in hand. We were sitting in a long line of vehicles full of people waiting to get into beautiful Canada. At the time, we didn't think we looked too different from anyone else. To be honest, though, if you got just the visual of my husband (minus the verbal interaction), all six foot clad in black leather and wearing dark glasses, your brain might easily go to Tony Soprano rather than gregarious pastor. Whatever it was, by the time our turn came, our officer already had a problem with us. The bike ahead of us had passed right through, so we felt good about that. We started getting the same questions over and over again. Then he started asking about how many weapons we had on the bike, and my husband again answered politely, none. The next question was about how many guns we owned. My husband might not have given the best answer here, but as any good southern boy would, he said off-handedly, "Every imaginable kind." So then he was told to tell what *kind* specifically. Fed up with playing by the rules and re-answering the same questions over and over, my husband decided it was time to pull out those people skills and add a little charm and humor—to no avail. To say it didn't work is putting it mildly. As you may have guessed, by this time humor had lost its magic. Every attempt at lightening the moment was met with more malice. We wiped the smiles off of our faces, and my husband turned his backward baseball cap around and gave two word answers: "Yes, sir," or "No, sir." Whatever it took to not have to unpack the whole bike for a search.

With one final, "Are you carrying any weapons, illegal drugs, or alcohol on the bike?" and one final very sincere "No, sir," we pulled away from the gate.

We stopped a little way up the road to put helmets on and take a deep breath, thankful to be in beautiful Canada. "What in the world was that about?" Cam asked.

"I don't know. You looked dangerous I guess," I replied. "Next time turn your Homeland Security cap around sooner. I think it helped."

Catching a glimpse of himself in the mirror, he asked, "Do you think it was these Smith & Wesson shooters glasses?" That realization started us laughing, and we were definitely ready to laugh again.

"Well, it's good to know we are in a safe country where they keep people like you *gun carriers* out," I said when I could catch a breath. Laughter is truly good for the soul.

My cute tough guy. He'll get them with the humor and charm next time. As every good comedian knows, sometimes it's just a tough crowd. My husband later told me that he was very well aware that humor does not work at border crossings in any country. These officials, he very seriously informed me, have been given a humor bypass. As far as I can tell, it somehow keeps the country safe. The things you learn as you travel.

"Let's celebrate!" he said.

"Whatever you want, my love. What do you want to do?" I replied. Come to find out he had googled Victoria Island, Canada, as well. To my great joy, our time did include a big king-size bed with feather pillows. Before we left the area, we strolled through the Empress Hotel's rose garden and enjoyed its civilized beauty. The ivy-covered stone walls, with the cabled roofline and turrets rising to the blue sky, gave us the perfect cultured moment before we hit the wild, wide-open spaces of Canada. When we went in to the restaurant to have tea served in china cups, our black leather once again seemed a little out of place. Maybe it was the glances we were getting that said we didn't look like "high tea" kind of people. But after five minutes of my husband's charm, the waitress and he had quite a friendship and we got the royal treatment.

Lessons Learned from the Back of a Harley

There are three lessons I learned while contemplating our story, mile after mile, on the Canadian highway. The first was that celebrating is a *must* for a healthy marriage. I realized that it had been a significant practice in our marriage. Second, laughter is essential for a good celebration, and third, I still want Cam to have the best half of the burrito. We'll get back to the burrito. On to the first lesson.

Cam and I have always been *people* people. We know the value of investing in relationships. We have a big family that we love very much, and we have a big church family that we cherish with all of our hearts. We celebrate life with reckless abandon: weddings, births, graduations, retirements, showers, birthday parties. If there is picnic, potluck, low-country boil, or BBQ, we're there. The problem was that having a fast-paced ministry with lots of people in our lives had a way of pushing certain relationships to the bottom of the pile—the *pile* of things to do and places to be. During any of the biggest celebrations of the year, my family was very aware that we wouldn't celebrate until we had made sure that thousands of other people had had a great celebration. The pile of things to do and places to be grew greater than our ability to stay connected. If you had ever told me as a newlywed that there would come a day when I couldn't tell you if my husband had clean underwear or anything for dinner that night, I wouldn't have believed you. That day came, and worse days followed. I would be asked by a friend in passing conversation where Cam was, and I often actually said, "Would you think I'm a bad wife if I said I'll have to check with his assistant to see which city he's in tonight?" She didn't have to answer—I already knew. My own pile of things to do had my mind too occupied.

We started regularly celebrating in our marriage to survive. If you look up the word *celebrate* in the dictionary, you can read these words: "To observe or commemorate with ceremonies or festivities ... to praise widely." We didn't just want to celebrate *in* our marriage; we wanted to *celebrate* our marriage—to give it a place of honor that we felt God intended for it to have in our lives. The first little tradition we started was to *date until death*. Cam's Christmas gift to me one year was to hand me his calendar so that I could pick two nights a month to hold for our date nights. This little ceremony of date night picking has continued for many years now. Some couples can fit in one date a week, but we were doing well to get two nights a month. I loved the job of bending both of our calendars to accommodate these dates.

Dating is full of all the right stuff. Someone has gone to the effort of planning something. You save the date and think about what you're going to wear. Sometimes the anticipation is half the fun. Most of all, it takes your relationship back to where it began when you were both saying to each other, "You are worth the effort." Dating has remained our non-negotiable tradition.

When you intend to celebrate something, you desire to make it known to other people. The dictionary description says, "praising it widely." I didn't know, until partway into the process, how important this part of celebrating was. My husband began to make it widely known that our dates would not be bumped on his calendar. He would say from the pulpit that couples should readjust their calendars and date nights should be sacred. We loved sharing and teaching that marriage should be honored on many levels as God designed it to be. God's plan for our marriage was both spiritual and physical. Celebrating both aspects gave our marriage a place of honor in our busy lives.

Laughter became a goal for every celebration. We learned lesson number two the hard way. I will confess I have always been a snooty laugher. I'd kind of put my nose in the air and look at you sideways as if to say, "This better be good. I don't laugh at just anything."

Being married to a very funny man, I would often be asked, "How can you not laugh at him? I'd be laughing all day long." Let's be honest: no one has heard more jokes, or the same jokes more times, than pastor's wives. As I sat in my predictable spot every Sunday, I would often have people tell me that they couldn't wait to see my reaction to Cam's jokes. Their favorite was the rolling eyes and shaking of my head, followed by, "The man is not right," for those close enough to hear. Yes, I realize how mean and unsupportive that sounds (that's why I am confessing).

It became even more obvious that I had this problem when I was diagnosed with breast cancer. After much reading to try to get my head around facing this dark season in my life, I came across some advice that was very helpful. The suggestion was to laugh every day as you go through treatment. There were many scientific reasons given that had to do with good things being released in your brain during laughter. However, my heart simplified it to a verse that my preschooler quoted like this: "A cheerful heart is like goooood medicine." That's his rendition of Proverbs 17:22.

Cam and I decided that I would take laughter breaks every day, just like medicine. Knowing what you do now about the kind of laugher I am, you realize he had his work cut out for him. I would get very intense some days as I read and worried and prayed. I would think to myself, *Nothing can make me laugh today. It's impossible.* But my husband would amaze me daily. The heights that man reached to pull out his best stuff—and more amusingly, the depths to which he plunged to make me laugh—will forever warm my heart. He would bring home silly or stupid stuff for us to watch and keep all the sad movies away. I had no choice. I just decided to be a laugher. It was either that or my husband was going to hurt himself trying to turn me into one. Settling my head on his chest, as his bass voice chuckled at whatever Barney Fife was saying, I found the release of great laughter. I'll never go back.

How long have you gone without laughing in your marriage? Believe it or not, you can go quite a while without realizing it. Throughout the many seasons of our marriage, we have learned to check ourselves with that question.

Laughter is essential to your marriage. However, if you wait until life is too intense, it can get to the place where it is too late to use it. Pull laughter out regularly and celebrate a little.

The last lesson that became abundantly clear to me on our little celebration adventure is that I still want Cam to have the best half of the burrito. I realize that talking seriously about a burrito doesn't make sense unless you know how seriously we take Mexican food in our house. My sons will still remind me of how I confused the poor waitress as we tried to divide the hot wings at our favorite Mexican restaurant when they were growing up. It was always essential to divide everything evenly, but we had the wrong number of wings, and I was smiling and trying to explain, "You know they always count."

I thought that explained everything quite clearly until she asked, "So you want me to bring two more hot wings?" I didn't see the problem. A normal family rule between the boys when dividing anything was one person split it or cut it and the other guy chooses which half he wants. That works well for brothers. However, when it comes to my honey, we have a different tradition.

My husband loves a big burrito supreme and all the trimmings. In our effort to be better in our eating habits, we have started to share. I realize now that I have to divide it and choose his half for him so he will get the good half. If I let him choose his half, he always gives me the good half. I heard him describe marriage for a group of young pastors once. He said, "There is always a good half of a divided burrito. You look at it, and it is exactly the way you like it. Then you realize you want her to have it. That's marriage!" That's my guy—wisdom and a way with words.

The dominant voices in our culture today are shouting that we need to take what we want to make ourselves happy. On the other hand, there is a still, small voice that continues to urge us to consider someone else before ourselves. That is the voice that I want to listen to. The strange thing is, I'm only happy when Cam gets the best half of that burrito. Even on this trip, as I was hoping he would gravitate to my kind of celebrating, it was refreshing to be reminded of that.

Celebration looks different to different people. Do you know how your husband likes to celebrate? Have you shared how you like to celebrate with him? Is celebrating for you relaxing or going wide open? Or is it a little of both? Sometimes after a long run of crazy schedules, we make plans to hide away. I found that it is better to talk about a plan than to leave the agenda in my mind. I'm not talking about a complicated plan here, just open communication. Keep it simple. Somebody starts, so I say something like, "I just want to keep my pajamas on all day, eat chocolate, and watch movies." His modifications are, "Great. Take away the pajamas and add a steak … it's a plan." The only rule is it has to be both people's idea of celebrating.

For us, celebrating can be simple and inexpensive. It has been for most of our marriage. The truth is, until this last trip, we had never been away from our church for over a month. These weeks away were a huge celebration for us. We enjoyed them because of the decision of some great church leaders who wanted to be sure my husband had a sabbatical after twenty-five-plus years in ministry. Sometimes it's not about frugality—it's about feasting.

Bible Backup:

Jesus walked this earth very simply. He modeled a life of servanthood and sacrifice. He lived in simple places and ate simple food. Although this was His lifestyle, He was not opposed to feasting as well as fasting. He had no place to lay His head some nights, and He stayed with rich friends at other times. When it was time for a wedding, He celebrated. When it was time to meet Matthew's lost friends, He joined the party. Our family discussions often turned in this direction as our sons were in college and seminary. One of our sons now just calls this his *feasting theology.* Ninety percent of the time, frugal and simple is the way to live. When you ponder this, it effects the way you think about many areas of your life, from your diet to your shopping habits. As we talked about in the previous chapter, this keeps in focus the real needs of life.

God Himself, however, set up a feasting plan to keep important things in focus so they would be remembered and honored. God clearly intended for marriage to be celebrated. The question is, do we truly believe this primary, God-designed relationship is a gift to us? Do we treat it as valuable as well as sacred? Maybe the best thing we could do during our Bible time this week is to remind ourselves of what God thinks about marriage.

Read the following scripture—God's opinion on honoring marriage:

"Marriage should be honored by all, and the marriage bed kept pure, for God will judge the adulterer and all the sexually immoral" (Hebrews 13:4).

God's opinion on how long marriage and marital love should last:

"May your fountain be blessed, and may you rejoice in the wife of your youth.

A loving doe, a graceful deer—may her breasts satisfy you always, may you ever be intoxicated with her love" (Proverbs 5:18–19).

The wisest man who ever lived gives his advice on how long marriage should be enjoyed.

"Enjoy life with your wife, whom you love, all the days of this meaningless life that God has given you under the sun—all your meaningless days. For this is your lot in life and in your toilsome labor under the sun" (Ecclesiastes 9:9).

Truth from this interesting perspective may sound strange, but it is good advice nevertheless. Solomon processes all that life has to offer from an earthly perspective, without God's understanding. His phrase "under the sun" is a repeated theme because that is the world he can see and understand. The word *meaningless* is often his conclusion for many things in this life. It is interesting that marriage is still at the top of the list of good things to experience in this meaningless life. Solomon had lived his life completely opposite of God's advice for a good marriage and never advises anyone to live that life. In fact, his writings are full of warnings concerning this. Which leads us to the third area where we need to seek God's opinion.

God's opinion on things that destroy marriage:

"You ask, 'Why?' It is because the LORD is the witness between you and the wife of your youth. You have been unfaithful to her, though she is your partner, the wife of your marriage covenant.

15 Has not the one God made you? You belong to him in body and spirit. And what does the one God seek? Godly offspring. So be on your guard, and do not be unfaithful to the wife of your youth.

¹⁶ "The man who hates and divorces his wife," says the LORD, the God of Israel, "does violence to the one he should protect," says the LORD Almighty.

So be on your guard, and do not be unfaithful" (Malachi 2:14–16).

Biblical Fact Check

Look up the verses below and write what God says about wives.

Genesis 2:24_____

Proverbs 18:22_____

Proverbs 19:14_____

1 Corinthians 11:3_____

I Corinthians 11:11–12_____

Ephesians 5:25_____

Ephesians 5:32_____

Ephesians 5:33_____

Colossians 3:18_____

Colossians 3:19_____

Titus 2:3–5_____

1 Peter 3:1 & 4–7_____

Personal Fact Check

So often in marriage we spend time evaluating if we feel loved. I found I had to start asking if I was bringing love into my marriage or if I was just expecting to receive it. To evaluate this, I went to the most beautiful description of love that I know.

Read I Corinthians 13:4–7 out loud:

"Love is patient, love is kind. It does not envy, it does not boast, it is not proud. ⁵It does not dishonor others, it is not self-seeking, it is not easily angered, it keeps no record of wrongs. ⁶ Love does not delight in evil but rejoices with the truth. ⁷ It always protects, always trusts, always hopes, always perseveres" (I Corinthians 13:4–7).

The first time I was encouraged to try the exercise below, I was not happy with what I found. It was eye-opening. I would like to encourage you to do the same. Fill in the blanks with your name. Then read it out loud.

I Corinthians 13:4–7

⁴ _____ is patient, _____
is kind. _____ does not envy,
_____ does not boast, _____
is not proud. ⁵ _____ does not
dishonor others, _____ is not
self-seeking, _____ is not easily
angered, _____ keeps no record of
wrongs. ⁶ _____ does not delight in
evil but rejoices with the truth. ⁷ _____
always protects, always trusts, always hopes,
always perseveres.

Which statements about love in I Cor. 13:4–7 seem most
incongruous to you as you read them with *your name*
substituted for "love"? Would those who are close to you
agree? What is the Lord telling you about this?
Journal your thoughts below:

_____

_____

_____

Marriages that last a lifetime are full of love. To be more exact, they are full of a love that is God-sized and God-powered. If you felt like you were falling short in that last reading, join the club. Don't, however, settle for a smaller, less potent love now that you have seen this picture. Lavish this kind of love on the man you chose as husband. Enjoy this husband of your youth. Honor your marriage as a couple daily, weekly, and seasonally with laughter and celebration. It's worth the effort.

Personal Evaluation:

Is your marriage something you have observed and commemorated with ceremonies or festivities—and praised widely? What could you do to begin celebrating your marriage without spending a dime? Maybe start with the last thing mentioned in the dictionary definition, and the most easily neglected: "praised widely." Write down something you could say to your husband to let him know how much you value your marriage and appreciate him. Start with telling him; then tell someone else when you have the opportunity.

Group Discussion Questions:

1. Describe the best celebration you have ever shared with your husband. Was it your engagement, wedding, anniversary, a special date, or a trip? How old were you both? Where were you? What was the occasion? How did you celebrate? Why do you think this was so special to you?

2. Describe your last date.

3. How have you readjusted *your* calendar—*your* agenda—to meet your husband more than halfway for time together, just the two of you? List a few specific things you could do to be more available to him.

4. Think of one aspect of your husband's personality that is unique or endearing, something you really enjoy or appreciate about his personality. What is it? Tell a little story that illustrates this aspect of his personality in action.

5. What kind of a laugher are you? A snooty laugher? A hearty laugher? A laugher who is always out of sync with everyone else? A howler or laugh-'til-you-cry

laugher? Explain. Feel free to use your own label. Would your husband and friends agree with your characterization?

6. Do you still want your husband to have the best half of the burrito? What language or image would you use to express the sacrificial nature of your love for your partner? Maybe it is something more like wanting him to have the Sunday afternoon nap, even if you don't get one; or wanting him to have the seat in first class, if only one of you can be upgraded; or serving him the last piece of cheesecake, and cheesecake is your passion! On the other hand, if the answer to this question is "no" or "I'm not sure," what do you think has changed in your relationship?

Recommended Reading: *From This Day Forward: Five Commitments to Fail-Proof Your Marriage* by Craig and Amy Groeschel

Biker's Trip Stats
&
Passenger's Log

*Starting/Ending Destination: Seattle, WA to Whistler, British Columbia, Canada (279 miles)

*Best Highways to Ride: Seattle Ferry Terminal; Seattle Bremerton Ferry Dock; WA-3 N; WA-104 W; US 101 N; Sequim Ave exit; Sequim-Dungeness Way; Dungeness Bay Blvd; Old Olympic Highway; US 101 N; Port Angeles-Victoria BC Ferry; TC-1; Highway-1A; TC-1N; Horseshoe Bay-Ferry; TC-1E; Highway 99

Bremerton, WA

*Don't Miss This:

USS Turner Joy Museum Ship

Puget Sound Navy Museum

Elandan Gardens

Bremerton, WA ... home of the Blackberry Festival

---

*Great Places to Eat:

Hi-Lo's 15th Street Cafe

Tony's Italian Restaurant & Pizzeria (great view of Oyster Bay)

Sequim, WA

*Don't Miss This:

Olympic Game Farm

Dungeness Spit

*Great Places to Eat:

Alder Wood Bistro

Port Angeles, WA

*Don't Miss This:

Salt Creek Recreation Area (hiking)

Olympic National Park (kayaking, hiking, etc)

*Great Places to Eat:

Café Garden (beautiful garden setting for breakfast, lunch, or dinner)

Victoria, BC, Canada

*Don't Miss This:

The Hartley Park Rose Garden

The Fairmont Empress Hotel (a legendary hotel frequented by kings and famous people). High Tea is at 4:00. C. S. Lewis fans only!

*Great Places to Eat:

White Heather Tea Room

Murchie's

> Cam Quote: Murchie's is an absolutely amazing place to buy English-style teas. I recommend #10 Downing blend!

> **We'll Be Back!**
>
> We'll Be Back ... Butchart Gardens is a beautiful group of floral displays. It's located in Brentwood Bay, which is near Victoria. It is a National Historic Site of Canada.

Horseshoe Bay, BC, Canada

*Great Places to Eat:

Boathouse Restaurants

Bay Moorings (great view of ocean and mountains)

Olive & Anchor Restaurant (great fish and chips with a view)

> So We Hear ... Red Fish Blue Fish has some of the best seafood in town. It is located right on the pier, which means there is not a lot of seating, but if you try one of their famous tacones (a grilled tortilla hand roll), it will be worth it!

Whistler, BC, Canada

*Don't Miss This:

Peak to Peak Gondola

Whistler Village

> Whistler, BC, Canada ... home of the Whistler Film Festival

*Great Places to Eat:

Splitz Grill

Cow's Whistler

Hy's Steakhouse

Ciao-Thyme

Delightful Detours:

Delightful Detours:
Maple Ridge - Paradise Café
(great homemade pie)

Worth the Trip ...

Horseshoe Bay is breathtakingly beautiful. It has the most waterfalls per mile of any road we've ridden.

CHAPTER EIGHT

Harley-Style Commitment

"Will this really be my job? I guess I
did say till death do us part."

—Me

Calgary, Alberta, Canada. What were we doing in Calgary and how did we get there? That's a story for another time. The beautiful city of Calgary, nestled in the foothills of the Canadian Rockies, was where this trip began. It was a sunny, cloudless July day, and we were thrilled to be there getting to know our neighbors to the north. My husband was perfecting talking like a Canadian and fitting right in. Big Red was on standby, looking superior. Sometimes it's hard having the best-looking bike. Shopping opportunities were abundant. I was spending my final minutes before gearing up trying to figure out the exchange rate between my US and Canadian dollars.

The city was built where two rivers merged together. Cityscapes were full of sweeping bridges spanning these rivers. If you looked across the rooftops in one direction, you would see snowcapped mountaintops against the sky. If you were to head out of the city in another direction, you would end up in miles and miles of prairie. I knew a little about this area because I had an aunt, two sisters, and a nephew who had attended a great missionary training school called Prairie Bible Institute located seventy-five minutes outside of Calgary. You could look out across the prairie for miles without even seeing a tree. It was hauntingly beautiful. On this day, however, as plans would have it, we were heading toward those snowcapped mountains.

The fun part about this trip is that we were traveling with some friends. It's always a good idea to travel with some cute young friends because as you look across the highway at them and wave, you say in your mind, *That's what we look like riding down the highway.* You travel on in denial, but you feel good about the day. Geared up and ready, with both bikes secured, we started down the Trans-Canada Highway 1 to the west. We were off with scarves flying behind us. Yes, you still need a scarf in July in Canada. I could tell exactly what my streaming scarf looked like as I glanced across at my friend.

Our goal for the day was to go to the town of Banff, through the Banff National Park, and ultimately to Chateau

Lake Louise. The topography started changing a few miles down the road, and more trees and rolling hills came into view, but it wasn't the scenery that captured our attention for the rest of this trip. It was the wildlife. I shouldn't have been surprised. Any time you travel through a national park, you have a better chance of seeing animals because they seem to know that they are in a safe place. I was still unprepared. We spotted stately elk with huge antlers grazing, and small foxes running the hills. We were whooping and giving each other the thumbs up as we pointed out something of interest and the other bikers witnessed it too. At one point there was a river to my left and an eagle swooping to my right. He would exert long, strong pulls with his wings that would allow him to glide for what seemed like minutes. He angled his wings to bank the curve, floated back across the highway, and effortlessly rode the wind back up the river. I watched in wonder. I couldn't believe that we were being given this gift. To be allowed to watch him for such a long time made me feel like I was being let in on a secret. My private glimpse into his world had my heart soaring for minutes after our beautiful eagle left us. I'm sure he had to check out another part of the river, and I had to get back to watching for our next wild creature.

I was contemplating how the small growth mixed with wild flowers along the roadside could possibly have some interesting animals roaming there. The taller trees up the slopes could also be hiding animals of another size. My thoughts were wandering wildly until something in my husband's actions caught my attention. My mind started backtracking. What did he just say? "Did you say we're out of gas?" I asked.

He answered, "No, not yet. I just want you to know if we get close to empty, we will need to flip this switch so we can alternate to our reserve tank of gas." Well, good to know. My thoughts started soaring faster than that eagle. *Will this be my job? Will it happen as we are taking a curve, leaning low? Will his hands need to stay on the handles at all times?* He proceeded to show me how to turn the switch the right way and how to check the gauges. My mind was still racing with questions. *Do I know what he just said? Can I even hear him well enough to learn this lesson right now?* And the big question: *What is it going to take to get my body around to the front of his body and turn that switch while going sixty-five miles an hour down the highway?* It didn't appear to be anything I could reach from my current position. Now, I did remember seeing a movie where a girl was able to move around to the front of her motorcycle driver so she could be facing backward and shoot the bad guys. It seemed to me that even if I was able to do that maneuver, I would still be facing the wrong way for the task at hand. Maybe I was overthinking this. Do you think?

I was back to the first question again. *Will this really be my job? I guess I did say, "For better or worse," and, "Till death do us part!" Maybe I should just do what I can do and pray for a gas station.* When the gas station finally appeared, I knew we were going to have quite a bit to talk about.

As it turned out, our friends started talking first. "What in the world were you doing back there? Did you see the bear? We were flagging you like crazy."

"What bear?"

"The one right back there on the side of the road. He wasn't even up in the woods at all. You had to see him. It was a big grizzly bear! He was huge." They talked over each other excitedly.

Now, I'm not sure how well our friends can tell one species of bear from another. So maybe it wasn't a grizzly bear. But I'm pretty certain their bear recognition skills are intact. All I could think about was missing that bear. "Honey, we missed the bear!" I wasn't about to tell our friends that we were having a gas tank switching lesson when a huge bear was making his appearance. I lamely added to their second excited replay about the bear, "We saw the eagle." In my mind, I was vowing, *From this day forward, nothing will distract me from seeing a bear.*

I thought that by sheer determination I would make another bear appear. I scanned every clearing and peered behind every copse of trees. I grumbled a little out loud and pouted a lot silently. I never saw my Canadian bear. I have to say, however, that there was no disappointment in all we witnessed next. I had nothing left to wish for once we reached Lake Louise.

We enjoyed a stop in the town of Banff. We strolled the shop-lined street, with its welcoming cafes, but couldn't stay long. We were anxious to be back on our forest-lined road heading for those snowcapped mountaintops.

As Lake Louise came into view, it seemed that all of nature was pointing to her beauty. The rugged mountains that formed the lake basin jutted high behind her and formed a perfect V that guided every eye to their gem: a lake so serene and gentle in the midst of wild beauty. The blue color seemed almost otherworldly. I knew I had never seen something quite that true blue before. Protective arms of green surrounded her sides and held her in place. Even the regal mountain peaks visible beyond the V seemed to be bowing to her beauty. To make the whole picture perfect, there was one bright red canoe floating alone on the water's flawless blue surface.

There is a scientific explanation for the color of the water. It has something to do with the run off from the glaciers above that fill the lake. I tend to believe that God's perfect color palate once again painted something that we human artists can only dimly mimic. It is a turquoise blue, but not the flashy color that surrounds islands in southern waters. It is more like a piece of true turquoise mined out of the western mountains, with rich veins running through the gem. Let's just say if we could recreate it, we would put bowls and vases of this color on our tables and swirls of it in our drapes to adorn our windows. Surrounded with the perfect shade of chocolate brown, there would be nothing left to do but just sit back and breathe in the comfort of the room. As it is, I will just have to leave that feeling where it can truly be experienced: sitting beside Lake Louise.

We took a whole day to enjoy this spot. We walked her shores and hiked above her to get a better view. We spent the night there and regretted that morning would come and we would have to leave. The morning light only heightened the beauty of this sparkling gem. My brain still carries vivid pictures of beautiful Lake Louise and probably always will.

We had a big day of riding ahead. Within minutes of our departure, it started to snow. Did I mention that fun fact about Lake Louise? Any month of the year, you could experience snow at the base of the glaciers. We rode through snow, sleet, rain, and sunshine. We felt like the US Postal Service. It didn't matter what came next; we were going to ride through. It was time to get home, after all. Our final destination would be Somers, Montana, and family—who, to this day, my husband, in his loving wit, still refers to as "your people."

Our trek home would guide my mind through many memories. We traveled through places that had been a part of my childhood. The bridge over the Kootenay River is the actual place where I had to answer that proverbial question that every father asks his child, "If your brother told you to jump off the Kootenay Bridge, would you do it?" It was such an obvious *no* with the Kootenay Bridge looming above a plummeting fall to the river. I still don't think I have ever seen another bridge that high. It was the picture in my brain every time I thought about *choosing right* for myself. Lesson learned.

We crossed back into the States and started seeing signs with the poor, hungry horse on them. I remembered being worried about this horse during my childhood. It turns out that through adult eyes, Hungry Horse, Montana, is a pretty place to travel through and not really that scary at all. The ride from Libby, Montana, to Somers is one I had taken many, many times as a child. It led from my house to my grandparent's house. There was just something magical about the road that took us there. Every trip ended the same way: all of our voices from the back of the station wagon giving the cry, "I see Grandma's lake first!" An argument would ensue to see if we could determine the actual winner of the lifelong game.

Big Red took the final curve with grace, and I shouted the long-practiced line in my husband's ear. He had the nerve to claim that he had seen Grandma's lake first. I was too excited to argue. We were here! There would be several more curves to navigate before we would have the full view, but each one revealed a little more of the lake's beauty. We rounded the last bend and saw my lake shining in all of its glory. Finally releasing the breath that had been trapped in my lungs, the words "I'm home" escaped.

Lake Louise will always be a wonder in my memory, but this was home, my lake and my first love. I have yet to see a lake that can steal my heart away. It has another name, but I hesitate to tell you what it is. Many small towns are nestled along its shores, and our small town is called Somers. My dad and his siblings were raised on the lake, and we cousins would return home with regularity to Grandma's lake for birthdays and holidays. Now our children and their cousins are drawn home to Grandma's lake to stay connected with each other and to let their children get acquainted. Some places just seem to have a way of wrapping warm arms around many people and letting them know they are *home*.

This place is where I witnessed marriages that could last a lifetime. Through layers of generations, I saw people who said, "For better or worse, you're my person." The lessons that taught my heart were played out in dozens of small ways. A woman who served many tirelessly and still took a quiet walk to the woodpile with a jar of cold water for one man. She baked for many but made sure he got to taste the bread while it was still warm. A piece of pie was saved aside so he wouldn't miss out. The funny thing is I saw those things when I was five, and then saw them again just last year at the family reunion. The faces and the loving hands had changed, but the message was still the same: you're my person. His old hands fixing her glasses with a tiny screwdriver and then testing to see if they fit just right. Young hands lifting a baby off her hip because he sees she's getting weary. Each small thing making a declaration without a word: I'm here for the whole ride.

Through the years of our marriage, my husband has loved this place—I think as much as I have. Yet it never fails ... as we arrived *home* that day, my heart was brimming with all of the things I wanted him to experience while he was there: a trip out to Viking Island on the boat to find the perfect diving rock; big loud, long, storytelling at crowded dinner tables; picking purple and yellow cherries right off the trees and eating them. But most of all, I wanted him to experience something that would tell him, "You're my person. You always will be."

Lessons Learned from the Back of a Harley

From the beginning, God walked in the garden, teaching His first children about life by showing them the wonders He had created. Jesus taught deep truth while holding up a grain of wheat, and urged His students to consider how it had to die to bring life. Or He held up a mustard seed while telling listeners to look and consider moving that mountain. Nature has a way of showing us God's truth in clear pictures. This kind of teaching always turns your heart and mind from creation to the Creator. If He took such great care with a lake or a mountain, think of the care He used as He created you.

I waxed poetic about lakes and mountains that I love in this chapter because nature has always had some lessons for me. I would be remiss if I did not clarify that each place is special because of the people I experienced life with there. My lake can only be home because of the people who, for generations, determined to make it home. It is the kind of commitment that says, "I will always be here. You can always come home because I'm not going anywhere." This kind of commitment will make our marriages strong. This is the kind of commitment that travels though snow, sleet, and rain to get to the sunshine of *home*.

The lesson of this kind of commitment is what we need to unpack in this chapter.

Commitment starts with a *decision* you make before you walk down the aisle and say, "I do." Commitment is a *declaration* you make the day you stand at the altar and promise, "For better or worse," and, "Until death do us part." Commitment is also something you *confirm* daily. You ratify your decisions and declarations from this day forward, every day, for the rest of your marriage.

There is nothing like good old-fashioned commitment. It is undervalued in a culture like ours, in which we want things fixed fast. If things can't have a fast fix, we opt for a different route. Cam and I are often asked what made our marriage last and endure the hard times. Our answer is usually simple. We committed to this marriage until one of us dies.

Commitment

- **A Decision:** We decided we were going to take our marriage seriously. We decide that divorce would not be an option for us. We decided that this was for life.

- **A Declaration:** We declared before God and the family and friends gathered that we would hold tightly to each other during the better and worse seasons. We promised each other that we would not speak the word *divorce* in our home as a threat or answer to our problems.

- **A Daily Confirmation:** From this day forward, we are going to live as if the above decisions and declarations are true. This is played out in hundreds of ways as we decide to put our declarations into actions.

Our lessons can be best looked at in three categories:

1. **From this Day Forward**: Commitment is something that can start today, regardless of what has gone on in the past. God is always ready to forgive and restore. If you are single, married, divorced, or remarried, you are able to start from this day forward to have a God-sized commitment to marriage.

    Singles–Learn now how seriously God feels about marriage before you decide on a spouse and declare you will be together for life.

Married and Remarried–The marriage that you are in now is the marriage to which God wants you to commit. Find ways to confirm daily that you are in for a lifetime.

Divorced–Let God's forgiveness and healing do a work in your life. He can make all things new. My family, like yours, is full of all kinds of marriages. I shared in the story section what I learned from the marriages that lasted a lifetime. I have also learned from watching the second marriages that have a God-sized commitment to protect their marriage. The destructive forces that led to divorce the first time are lessons learned and not allowed in. If you have been divorced, it is still possible for you to have a strong, Godly marriage.

2. **For Better or Worse**: Commitment is what sees you through the bad times as well as the good. It works when your marriage is barreling down the highway at sixty-five miles per hour and there are all kinds of things coming your way. Some are good and exciting and some are a threat to you. It's the better or worse

mentality that will see you though both. There are times when the only thing you should focus on is what will keep you safely moving down the highway. So you focus on having enough gas and you miss the grizzly bear. Our tendency is to say, "Is this my life … is this really my job?" and the answer is, "Yes." It's not flashy and exciting, but it is your job because it will get your family safely through. At this stage in my marriage, I can't name one flashy or exciting thing that would have been worth my family crashing.

3. **Till Death Do Us Part:** Your marriage can make it to the end! God designed a relationship that would withstand the winds of time. He designed a relationship that would actually be strengthening to you and see you through the storms of life. Too often, however, we allow time to batter this relationship with neglect, and the storms of life that rage are our marriages. When our marriages are no longer the port in the storm, they have stopped being what God intended.

The lesson I learned on the back of a Harley is that you can make it through more snow than you think. You can make it through more sleet than you feel is humanly possible. If you stick together, you can stand getting colder and wetter than you think you can and still survive because the sunshine is coming. Most of all, you won't ever want to stop going down that road because it is taking you to the safe place called home.

Bible Backup:

We are going to be focusing on two different thoughts as we look into scripture. **The first thought** *is that we can change our lives by changing our mind.*

Read Romans 12:1–2 below and underline the phrases related to life change:

Therefore, I urge you, brothers and sisters, in view of God's mercy, to offer your bodies as a living sacrifice, holy and pleasing to God—this is your true and proper worship. ² Do not conform to the pattern of this world, but be transformed by the renewing of your mind. Then you will be able to test and approve what God's will is—his good, pleasing and perfect will.

Read Philippians 4:8 (ESV) below and underline the kind of things we should be thinking about:

> [8] Finally, brothers, whatever is true, whatever is honorable, whatever is just, whatever is pure, whatever is lovely, whatever is commendable, if there is any excellence, if there is anything worthy of praise, think about these things.

It's interesting that Romans 12:1 tells us to give our physical bodies to God. This means give our actions and the things we do to God. But verse two holds the secret to doing that. It will take a renewing of our minds before we will ever decide to do the right things. It is the only way we can know what is "good, pleasing and perfect" for our marriage. If we want to change our marriages, we need to change our minds. As Paul tells us in verse two, the world loves to control how we think.

The second thought *that we want to process is that other people's thinking and lives can change when Scripture* *changes us. Read about the early church in the Scripture below and think about the underlined phrase.*

42 They devoted themselves to the apostles' teaching and to fellowship, to the breaking of bread and to prayer. 43 Everyone was filled with awe at the many wonders and signs performed by the apostles. 44 All the believers were together and had everything in common. 45 They sold property and possessions to give to anyone who had need. 46 Every day they continued to meet together in the temple courts. They broke bread in their homes and ate together with glad and sincere hearts, 47 praising God and enjoying the favor of all the people. And the Lord added to their number daily those who were being saved. (Acts 2:42–47)

What do you think was meant by "all the people"?

_____

_____

_____

The early church was immersed in and surrounded by the Roman culture. It looked very much like our modern culture from a morality standpoint. If the people living in Roman times had that kind of response to the church and the way they lived, is it possible that we could be having that same reaction from people watching us today? How desperately do the people around you need to see a marriage that is different—not one that gets its teaching from the world but one that gets its teaching from the scriptures?

First Peter 2:9 and Titus 2:14 both talk about God's people being "peculiar" in some of the more literal translations. I think that is a good way to be described. I hope and pray that we start standing out more in our marriages every day. I was visiting with a young family in the parking lot at church, listening as the kids were giving the age old argument that none of the other kids had to do what their family had to do. I told them with a chuckle that it was a lot better to grow up in a weird family. The Huxfords liked being strange; we didn't want our family to be just like everyone else. They finally agreed it was cool to be weird, and the mom gave me the silent thank you look. It's not always easy to be a peculiar people, but it is always good.

Biblical Fact Check

> [8] Finally, brothers, whatever is **true**, whatever is **honorable**, whatever is **just**, whatever is **pure**, whatever is **lovely**, whatever is **commendable**, if there is any **excellence**, if there is anything worthy of **praise**, think about these things. (Philippians 4:8 ESV)

Journal your thoughts about each of the bold words as it applies to things in your marriage. Ask, for example, "What is true about my marriage?"

_____

_____

_____

Personal Fact Check

> [8] Finally, brothers, whatever is **true**, whatever is **honorable**, whatever is **just**, whatever is **pure**, whatever is **lovely**, whatever is **commendable**, if there is any **excellence**, if there is anything

worthy of **praise**, think about these things. (Philippians 4:8 ESV)

Journal your prayers for your marriage here. Mention each of the bold words in your prayers. Paul tells us to "think about these things," but what keeps your mind from focusing on these good things? Write a prayer in your journal about that. Come back to these pages in the days to come and remind yourself of the prayers you are praying for your marriage.

_____

_____

_____

Well, girls, our time together is almost over. I hope you will keep the discussions flowing with your spouse and your Christian sisters. I pray you will continue to urge one another on in the good fight for your marriage. Can I just say in my final words to you that whatever you do to strengthen your marriage will bless you, and, believe it or not, the people around you? There are generations coming after us that need to see a God-designed marriage. I want my granddaughters to have a picture of what a lifelong marriage can look like. They will need to watch it from the time they are five until they are fifty to get it right. Those of you taking this seriously will be their picture. Thank you.

Recommended Reading: *As Long as We Both Shall Live: Experiencing the Marriage You've Always Wanted* by Dr. Gary Smalley and Ted Cunningham

Biker's Trip Stats
&
Passenger's Log

*Starting/Ending Destination: Calgary, AB, Canada to Somers, MT (420 Miles)

*Best Highways to ride: Trans Canada Highway/ AB 1 W; AB 93S; BC 93 S; MT-40E; US-2W; US-93S;

Calgary, AB Canada

*Don't Miss This:

Stephen Avenue Mall

Calgary Stampede

*Great Places to Eat:

Smuggler's Inn

Buchanan's

Ed's Restaurant

Calgary, AB Canada ... home of the Calgary Stampede

We'll Be Back:

Calgary Stampede is a rodeo, exhibition, and festival that is held in Calgary every July. It's one of the largest rodeos in the world. This event has it all, from a parade to concerts, shows, and so much more.

Banff, AB, Canada

*Don't Miss This:

Ice Magic Festival

Banff AB, Canada ... home of the Ice Magic Festival

*Great Places to Eat:

Eddie Burger

The Grizzly House

Lake Louise, AB, Canada

*Don't Miss This:

Banff National Park

Icefields Parkway

Kootenay National Park

(beautiful scenery)

Lake Louise, AB, Canada ... home of the Western Heritage Jubilee

So we hear ... Moraine Lake is located in Banff National Park and is glacier-fed. The views are stunning since it is located in the Valley of the Ten Peaks.

*Great Places to Eat:

The Post

Deer Lodge

Lake Louise Railway Station and Restaurant

Catch it on the next trip: Icefields Parkway runs from Lake Louise, through two national parks (Banff and Jasper) and ends in Jasper, AB, Canada. It runs parallel to the Continental Divide and is known for its beautiful scenery.

Kootenay National Park has breathtaking natural beauty, from snow-covered mountatops to rushing waters.

Hungry Horse, MT

***Don't Miss This:**

Huckleberry Patch Cannery

> Hungry Horse, MT ... home of the
> annual Huckleberry Festival

***Great Places to Eat:**

Elkhorn Grill

Somers, MT

> Somers, MT ... home of the Cajun
> Street Dance Festival

***Don't Miss This:**

Flathead Lake (the largest natural freshwater lake in the western

part of the contiguous United States)

US Route 93 (scenic drive with great views of Flathead Lake)

> Kalispell, MT ... home of the annual
> Glacier Jazz Stampede

Kalispell, MT

***Great Places to Eat:**

Norms News (great buffalo burger)

Sykes (amazing homemade cinnamon buns every morning ...

don't ask me how I know!)

Capers

Bullman's Wood Fired Pizza

Delightful Detours:
Bigfork, MT (chosen as "One of the Fifty Great Towns of the West")

Worth the Trip:

Glacier National Park has amazing animal sightings and sweeping views. Kids can also be seen playing in the glaciers in August.

Printed in the United States
By Bookmasters